HONORARY
DOG

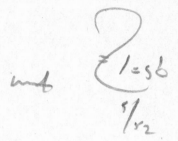

HONORARY DOG

Dora Wright

Being some anecdotes and reflections from fifty
years of living and working with dogs

line drawings by Julie Styles

W.H. ALLEN · LONDON
A Howard & Wyndham Company
1983

Copyright © Dora Wright, 1983

Typeset by Phoenix Photosetting, Chatham, Kent
Printed and bound in Great Britain by
Mackays of Chatham Ltd, Kent
for the Publishers, W.H. Allen & Co. Ltd,
44 Hill Street, London W1X 8LB

ISBN 0 491 03370 2

To my parents

'. . . long association with the species had made
her a sort of honorary dog herself.'

P. G. Wodehouse ('The Go-getter', *Blandings Castle*)

Contents

PART ONE:
Having

Take what you want, says God,
And pay for it . . . I've paid.
I've paid in money, effort, comfort, time:
In broken flowers, in crumpled, mud-stained clothes,
In trampled carpets , sleepless nights, in rage;
And in that bitter moment at the end,
When on the table, circled in arms of love,
With gentle, grateful eyes, she glides at last
Into her endless sleep.

I've paid. What have I taken
Worth all this price of ruined chairs, ripped books,
Chewed shoes and soon-forgotten crime on crime?
I've taken lives that centred all on me.
I've taken joy and laughter for my tears,
With dividends of friends, and hopes and fears.
I've taken love, and walked as one bewitched,
Safe through life's snares, while I gave thought
To lustrous eyes, to brilliant coats, to forms
That spring and leap and run, enchanted beings,
Taking my spirit with them as they fly.

And when the reckoning's made on my last day
Of all my foolish work and lack of thrift,
Whether in debt or credit it will stay –
I'll not have bought, for no price buys a gift.

1
Vocation

Why does anyone become so involved with one subject that it absorbs all their interest and can even change their life? Why choose one thing and not another? Manias are as various as the human race. Mine has been for dogs from my earliest remembrance and its origin is too obscured in the shadows of childhood for me to be able to identify it with any certainty.

Perhaps all monomanias spring not from the objects themselves but from the personalities of their devotees. These personalities in turn are formed at least in part by events (sometimes apparently unimportant events) which have happened to their owners. This could explain why the strongest enthusiasms are often formed fairly late in life, after such influences have had time to work on the person involved.

But I literally can't remember a time when I wasn't hypnotized by dogs, so if my theory is right, what could these influences have been in my own case? To begin with, both my parents were fond of dogs and believed that children ought not to be brought up without them. So there must always have been a dog present as a valued member of the family circle even in my earliest infancy, and I expect that as for most small children the differences in kind were rather fuzzy to me at that time so that I would have looked on the resident dog as merely a different shaped but friendlier brother.

My first true memory of a dog – a memory out of my own head and not a picture drawn there by repeated verbal accounts from other people – is of a rough-haired fox terrier named Jack. I must first say that we were a large family indigenous to Bermondsey in South East London, with a social circle consisting almost exclusively of various aunts and uncles and their own numerous families of cousins. Christmas and similar occasions were celebrated by large and prolonged parties.

One of my uncles was an alcoholic as a result of having received head injuries during the 1914–18 war, and in this my first doggy memory he is lying dead drunk under our parlour table with beer drooling from his open mouth. People are laughing indulgently, but I am crying because Jack is licking at the trickling beer and for some reason this fills me with horror and I am under the table with them trying to pull him away. I get into such a state between revulsion and indignation that my mother intervenes, Jack is put outside the room and I am picked up and quietened. My uncle is picked up too, tidied, wiped, and propped up in a comfortable chair to sleep it off.

Strange to say I have absolutely no other memories or knowledge of Jack – where he came from, how old he was or what happened to him. Yet the passion with which I reacted to this incident was very likely the strongest emotion I had ever felt till then in my short life. It left me feeling that dogs needed *looking after*, and that even grown-ups couldn't always be depended upon to see that they got it. I also remember Jack's trim, well-muscled shape, and that it made me feel even then that he was a truly noble creature. I certainly compared him favourably with my poor drunken uncle. It was probably this incident with Jack which gave me a distaste for these family 'knees ups'. When they were held at our house I always tried to sneak out to the back kitchen where the dog and cat were exiled – very unfairly, I thought. This annoyed my mother, who accused me of being unsociable. Sometimes I was ordered back into the parlour. I went with a poor grace and usually slid back into the kitchen again, not without some booty in the shape of a handful of toffees or nuts to make my trip worthwhile, and by cuddling down to the dog in his bed often avoided recapture by being unnoticed or just shamming sleep when anyone passed through.

Looking back I seem to have spent most of my early years on the floor with the dog, or with the cat if we had no dog at the time. I never sat on a chair if I could help it. The floors were covered with linoleum and scrubbed with strong carbolic soap once a week. We had no carpets but there were a good many rugs, mostly rag rugs bought in the street market, at the door, or home-made. Vacuum cleaners were then not available to the *hoi polloi*. My mother used to take up 'the mats' and shake them out of the back door, sweep the floor and replace them. As our animals were seldom wormed after their first birthday I feel I ought to have contracted toxocariasis, the round-worm disease about which such an almighty fuss has been made in recent years. Weekends and holidays I spent in Southwark Park, then quite overrun with dogs both stray and accompanied, and was never happier than when picnicking or turning somersaults on its tainted soil. Yet when I participated in the dogbreeders blood test for toxocariasis at Windsor Championship Show in 1977 my result was negative. I felt quite cheated, but at least I am a walking testimonial to the fact that this disease is a lot harder to contract than is popularly supposed.

My parents had seven children. One older than myself died as a baby before my arrival. I was number six, but my baby sister also died before I was seven years old. My mother was heartbroken by the death of this enchanting little daughter at the age of two and a half. The terrible shock and sorrow brought on a nervous breakdown, but

11

for the mother of five other children there could not be the relief of a collapse. Somehow she must carry on, and somehow she did, through what must have been years of dragging physical and mental misery.

I was now the youngest by nearly five years. My brothers ignored me as much as possible, and my eldest sister disapproved of my tomboy tendencies and tried to hector me into behaving 'like proper children do'. Nell, my other sister, was later to become very close to me, but at this period I remember her most as mercilessly teasing me. I expect she also was missing our mother's accustomed attentions. Anyway I suffered a good deal from this cause and know from first hand experience how much misery can result from this unpleasant pastime.

Being the youngest child can be a lonely position, and my mother was too overburdened with work and unhappiness to take as much trouble with me as she otherwise would have done. I knew even at the time that I was getting away with a lot of things, and I knew why, yet childlike I couldn't help taking advantage of this state of affairs. I was an obnoxious child, but lonely I also was, so I got a good deal of comfort from the family dog. In spite of her very real troubles my mother knew this, and so she and my father didn't discourage my excesses in this direction as they otherwise might have done.

I grew older, my mother slowly recovered, my sister ceased to tease and became a friend. I was happier, but by now my emotional dependence on the dog was well established and was beginning to come from the dog as well as from within myself. I didn't make friends very easily, in fact I had a sizeable inferiority complex and found I could face life a lot better with a dog beside me. Confidence was one of the first and most valuable gifts I gained from this partnership.

I suppose that during my childhood I did think about other things besides dogs, but I can't remember what. Not that we were very lucky with our dogs. We had a succession of them, separated by dogless wastes like deserts.

I remember there was a beautiful bookshop in the Jamaica Road where the kindly but probably misguided proprietor allowed grubby little me to sit at his lovely refectory tables and look at his wonderful books. One terrible day when a beloved dog was in extremis, I went to him as the only person I knew who owned a telephone and begged him to phone for a vet.

He did, and I went home, but the vet did not come and the dog died. I had to go back to the bookseller and ask him to cancel the vet, and there in front of a customer I wept buckets onto his tweed shoulder. The customer had gone by the time I recovered. I went too, and am ashamed to say that I never visited the bookshop again: the whole thing had been too traumatic and I couldn't bear it.

Soon afterwards the bookshop closed down. People said it was too good for the neighbourhood, but I always had a sneaking belief that its failure was all my fault.

The dog who had died was an Airedale named Jim, the gentlest thing that ever breathed. We had acquired him at the age of ten months, a trembling skeleton who flew cowering into the nearest corner at the sight of a broom. We only had him a year, and with hindsight I believe he was suffering from tuberculosis. Although I never trimmed him, being then only ten years old, he was in a way responsible for launching me on my career.

He was left in the care of friends when we went on holiday, and unknown to us children Dad had asked them to get him trimmed while we were away. It must have been done on the morning of our return, and we were heartbroken to be greeted by an elephant-blue naked creature with rough bristly skin and great black eyes burning in his shaven skull. This is known as 'scalping' although we didn't know the term then. Lamentations were soon over in the joy of reunion, but I never forgot the grisly sight, and that was the last time in all my life that anyone else has trimmed one of my dogs.

Poor Jim died before another trim was needed, and after two more dogless wastes divided by the short happy life of another Jim who was poisoned before he was twelve months old, my father gave me a brand new Airedale puppy for my thirteenth birthday. I named him Scamp, for I felt that Jim had proved an unlucky name, and resolved that he should be a superdog. He didn't let me down, and when his coat needed 'something done about it' I remembered poor Jim and resolved to trim him myself.

2
Scamp

Scamp was only five weeks old when my father and uncle picked him from the litter, and so small that he could sit comfortably on my father's hand. Pure bred if unpedigreed, he was one of ten puppies born in a barrel in a Deptford back yard. Dad paid twenty-five shillings for him – a full five shillings more than was being asked for his brothers, and he certainly justified it because he lived for over fourteen years and hardly ever had a day's illness. He was never inoculated either, for we were advised that the vaccines then available were so unreliable as to be often worse than the disease, although I do not know if this was true.

Scamp was so trainable. On his first birthday I wrote down a list of all he knew: so many names, so many commands, so many words. It came to over a hundred, and these words and commands could be used in combinations with every success. For instance, take the command Fetch, the noun Ball and the location Kitchen – I could say

'Fetch your ball – it's in the kitchen' and he would dash at once to the kitchen and come back with the ball. Or alternatively I could send him into the garden for a stick or down the road to meet my sister.

He was a great water dog, and after we had moved from Bermondsey I used to take him to Keston Common and put his ball down on the lakeside path, then walk him round to the other side of the water before sending him to fetch it. He would swim across to it, then swim back with it, often bringing my heart into my mouth when he got into the waterlilies or too near the swans. But he always came safely and triumphantly to shore.

Many years later I met a man who turned out to be the nephew of the people who owned Scamp's father. He told me that when this dog, Mick, was young his owner used to take him on summer evenings to Cherry Garden Pier to swim. Mick used to go off the end of the pier and swim the Thames right over to the Wapping side, where he would root about a bit before swimming back. How I wish I had seen that! But it must have happened while I was very young, for Mick was eleven when Scamp was born – only two years younger than myself, in other words. As Scamp lived to be fourteen, father and son together spanned a quarter of a century, which I think is truly remarkable.

Mick was a much dreaded fighter and known to have killed several dogs. His owner told me that Scamp was the split image of him when he was young, and I was anxious that he shouldn't begin fighting too. By getting him used to free play with other dogs from puppyhood I avoided this, but he went further than I anticipated – he became a one-dog police force. He just did not allow fighting. When a knot of dogs in the park were about to start a scrap he would walk, tiptoe, rigid and snarling, backwards and forwards between them until they gave up. On many occasions he actually broke up fights by crashing into the combatants to separate them, then implementing his cooling-down routine until all was calm. He never ever began a fight, and would avoid fighting if he could. Occasionally however, he was attacked by lunatics of the if-it-moves-

16

kill-it sort, and he was always the victor. His technique was to turn the attacker over on to its back with a swift blow of his paw, then to keep it there with his teeth bared at its throat until it signalled surrender. Then he would stand back and let it go, completely unmarked and only anxious to get as far away as possible.

I was fifteen and Scamp two when we moved to Petts Wood, and as we were some way from the National Trust woods I trained him to run with my bicycle. Without a lead, of course, for that is illegal, but he kept pace beautifully, running on the pavement half a length ahead of me. I let him set the pace so that I didn't overtax him. When I wanted to turn left I said 'Corner', when right, 'Heel', and he would leave the pavement to run by my left pedal. He never came into the road when we met parked cars or other obstructions, but trotted steadily on to emerge when they were past with a triumphant grin at me on our reunion.

Neighbours seeing us warned me that I would not be able to take him out by myself as there was a half-bred Alsatian living round the corner which brooked no other large dog anywhere on his patch. The first time I saw him I warned Scamp that there was a dog coming – he was busy with an interesting smell and this was an arrangement we had. He needed no more. He pulled himself up into the military pose which made him so much a chip off the old block – Mick the Battler all over again. Bonzo came to an abrupt halt, and as Scamp began his tiptoe mincing walk towards him, head high, the bully faltered, then crossed the road and passed by on the other side! And that set the pattern for the next ten years. These two redoubtables never came within yards of each other, and all beholders were much amazed at my dog's immunity from the dreaded Bonzo, who continued to beat up every other male dog in sight!

About this time we took Scamp on holiday to a remote Welsh farmhouse. On the first evening we climbed the hill to watch the sunset, and as Scamp ran ahead a bunch of sheep suddenly jumped bleating from the bracken at his feet. Instinctively he went to give chase, but as I yelled his name he turned and looked at me. 'No!' That was all he needed, and the sheep were safe. So were the very hens that wandered into the sitting-room to pick up the crumbs that fell from the table underneath which he lay.

While we still lived in Bermondsey he had a special friend. This was a very handsome Welsh collie named Jock, who belonged to Elsie, a girl a year or two younger than myself. We both went mad on 'training'. During the week we would teach our dogs what tricks we could think up – they would be found in no Obedience schedule today – and at weekends met to compare progress.

Jock was terribly gun-shy. The smallest crack or bang would set him running in blind panic, and he was often brought back from distant parts of London. On one occasion he failed to reappear and Elsie spent an agonising month with no news of him. One day I was cycling home from school and saw a dog which I thought was very like him. He was an unusually marked dog, coloured like a wolf-grey Alsatian (not merle) with silver paws and chest, pale yellow legs and lightly marked facial mask not unlike that of the Siberian husky. One never sees this colouring in the working collie now, and I wonder why – it was so attractive.

Anyway, I pedalled smartly up to the woman holding the other end of the lead and asked her if she had found the dog as my friend had lost one just like him. Oh no, she said, they'd had him for three months, her husband had had him sent down from the North. I spoke to him and he looked at me without enthusiasm, in fact he looked very dejected. The lady said that his name was Bob, which in sound of course is not unlike Jock, so that proved nothing.

But he certainly looked very much like Jock, so I asked her for her name and address and permission to bring my friend to see him. It amuses me now to remember that she promptly gave all three – I must have had a hypnotic eye like the Ancient Mariner. Anyway I cycled off full speed to Elsie's house to report to her and her mother. The latter was very dubious about my identification of the dog but gave Elsie permission to go round and satisfy herself.

As she had no bike I dropped mine in at home on the

way and picked up Scamp. I think I had some idea that he could make the identification positive, but it was due to his presence that I was denied admittance when we reached the woman's house, and so missed a scene which I would have given much to have witnessed.

Apparently Jock went crazy with delight when Elsie walked in – but according to the woman he greeted all visitors like that. So Elsie solemnly began to put him through all his tricks one after another, with the woman spluttering helplessly 'Yes, he does that – yes, my husband taught him that' and so on. The pièce de résistance was a magnificent trick which Elsie had dreamed up, in which the dog leapt madly round the room via the furniture without ever touching the floor until made to desist, which in this case was done by the woman, now fairly frantic but still not admitting anything.

Elsie thanked her gravely, then fetched her mother, post haste and highly indignant, and Jock was restored to the bosom of his rightful family.

However, in spite of the well-earned reputation for trainability which working collies have I truly believe that Scamp came out ahead in the weekly 'exams'. It brings tears to my eyes now to remember how proud I was of him. He was indeed my treasure and where my heart was. I lived to be with him and never got my fill of looking at him. He was really an obsession I suppose, but what a happy one. Although my family frequently got exasperated with 'you and that dog' and the inconvenient fact that it was my policy never to be separated from him for any other reason than school, still I believe he gave me more than I gave him.

Scamp was the first dog to teach me that dogs can recognise tunes, although I don't know why this should have surprised me, for what else is the whistle-recognition by which so many are trained to return? Anyway, 'Scamp's tune' was *Drink to Me Only with Thine Eyes*, which he could never hear without bursting into passionate wails and howls. It didn't matter how he heard it – whether we sang it or picked it out on the piano or whether it came over on the radio properly performed, the first few bars were enough to set him off.

The poor dog must have had a musical ear, for about this time I had my one attempt to play a musical instrument and chose the violin. Scamp made me give it up pretty quickly. He would lie flat on the floor and give tongue in tones of anguish as soon as I got it out of the case. This was one occasion on which my family were grateful to him for his influence over me. Unfortunately the disappearance of the violin from our home didn't finish Scamp's musical selectivity, and he embarrassed me horribly one day when passing a blind beggar playing the harmonica at the kerb. Once more he prostrated himself at the poor man's feet and gave of his best. I'm afraid I hurried off and only called him when I was well away and felt certain we could make our getaway safely.

Despite our closeness Scamp was most of all a family dog and my sister Nell and I loved him passionately as only children can. One of the times which brings him back most clearly to my recollection is Christmas.

Christmas for Scamp began with my mother making the Christmas puddings. He took a consuming interest in this activity because he knew it presaged a time of great excitement and good eating. We used to tease him with the remains of the lemons as they were squeezed into the mixture. We would dare him to take them. 'Here you are, Scamp, take it – it's *nice*.' He would stand his ground bravely as the lemon approached his nose, not moving his feet, but turning his head as far as he could, wrinkling his nose as the sharp smell assailed his nostrils. Then he would turn it the other way until he was forced to move, backing away with reluctant steps, and watering at the mouth like a Salvation Army trumpeter being baited in the same way by street boys. Then we would wickedly throw the lemon peel on to the floor and, unable to resist it, he would pounce on it and throw it up in the air, barely touching it by the skin of his teeth.

Scamp's favourite foods were toffee, cheese and coconut, and if he ever thought of Christmas I'm sure he thought of it in those terms. With more exotic foods abounding, cheese was at a discount, and my sister and I fed him a good deal on the sly. Toffees, of course, were a sort of foundation on which the sweet supplies were laid, and he seldom asked us in vain. As for coconut . . .

Being modern types we had no use for Christmas stockings but always used pillowcases. It amazes me now that our parents always managed to fill them. But when we had explored their contents and peeped at our books, it was Scamp's turn. He had a passion for undoing parcels, so all his presents were loosely wrapped in voluminous paper before being put into an old laundry bag. We held the neck open sufficiently for him to get his head and shoulders into it, and with wild snufflings he would bring out and disembowel one bundle after another. Sweets, cheese, discarded slippers, a lemon (don't worry, he saw the joke), a rubber mouse, a marrow bone, and best of all, his very own coconut, which spent at least half the day being used as a rugger ball before being opened and fed to him bit by bit.

We seldom bought him toys, for he had the habit of adopting unconsidered trifles himself. The best of these was a large brass knob off a derelict bedstead. By luck we found that a broken rolled-leather collar could be jammed securely in the hole to form a 'handle', and the thing became known as Scamp's Bomb. He delighted in coming up behind you very quietly and dropping it with a crash. With his luxuriant whiskers (which he had a habit of blowing through to emphasise important points in the conversation) and this infernal machine swinging in a sinister manner by the 'fuse', he looked a picture of the traditional and rather endearing Bolshie.

When we moved out of Bermondsey I explored the Kent countryside with him. With him I had holidays by the sea. He saw me at school, he saw me married and he saw my children. He must of necessity be always part of my development.

I suppose no dog is ever perfect and Scamp must have had some flaws for me to want to try some other breeds, but when I look back it is hard to remember them, for Scamp was a truly remarkable dog.

Since my father would not have any dog but an Airedale

I naturally grew up with a special feeling for and understanding of this breed. Most people seem to have a soft
spot for the breed they knew in their childhood, and some
never experiment with other breeds when they grow up
but remain constant to their early companions.

This can be a pity. Breeds are as varied as the needs of
different types of human beings. It may well be that the
dog that your parents kept is not nearly as well suited to
you personally as another which you have never tried. I
once knew an elderly lady who bred and kept spaniels all
her life until in her old age she became infirm and had to
give up her house with its kennels and exercising grounds
and go into a downstairs flat with a postage stamp garden.
She found good homes for her remaining dogs, but then
found she could not live dogless. So she bought a tiny grif-
fon. Although she had never previously been attracted to
the toy breeds she discovered that this minute bitch with
her vivacity, intelligence and charm gave her far more
than the spaniels. Of course for another person the
reverse could be true.

At all events I was eager to try a new pattern in dogs. In
spite of my early obsession with the species I still did not
really appreciate that breed can (and in fact should) deter-
mine the character of the dog almost as much as its shape.
I admired the beauty of the more glamorous breeds
perhaps excessively. I thought at that time that the Borzoi
was absolutely the last word in canine grace and glory. In
fact I spent some hours at the Natural History Museum
drawing the stuffed pair there preserved, and I still have
the sketch. Even now, although for the afficionado – and I
definitely am one – a really fine Airedale, fit and strong
and in the perfection of a show trim, is a glorious, indeed
a breathtaking sight, yet I can see that from the purely
visual angle he is outdone by such extravagant exhibition-
ists as the Borzoi, the chow, the standard poodle or the
Afghan hound.

I believed that a dog's character was almost wholly
made by the treatment and training it received from its
owner. Moreover I had an itch to try the other side of dog-
dom, the underprivileged and unpedigreed mongrel. This

was very ungrateful of me, because Scamp was just about as good a dog as ever lived.

Yet I felt I could have done better with him, that as my first real dog I had 'learnt' on him. I thought that if I could make a fresh start with a new puppy all the dog lore I now possessed would surely result in the production of a wonder dog to amaze all beholders. Such is vanity. Because I spent so much effort, time and thought on Scamp I believe I can take some of the credit for the success I had with him; but I never did better with any subsequent dog, and not as well, I fear, with most of them.

3
Diggaluggamunka – and Jane

My very next dog was a case in point. Wartime, a baby on the way and an acute shortage of money and most other things. What better time to indulge my hankering after a mongrel? I couldn't have afforded an Airedale even if I could have found one, and a small mongrel would take less feeding. On these two points at least Digger proved me right – he cost ten and six (52½p), and being not really a mongrel but a first cross between a working collie and a wire haired fox terrier, he existed quite comfortably on the scanty food made available by my own efforts and the generosity of a neighbour whose pocket made a little black market food available in sufficient quantities to allow her little girl to be choosy enough to leave some over for my dog.

Digger was a devastatingly attractive puppy, and I received several offers to buy him. Actually he had already had one home, where he had been badly neglected and much mauled by a horde of semi-savage young children. I used to see him trying to get a drink from the drainpipes, and when told he was for sale jumped at the chance. He was then four and a half months old.

Digger was brilliantly coloured. Blue black, red tan, with a dazzlingly silver jabot, four silver feet and a silver tip to his bushy tail which we said was his way of obeying the injunction to 'wear something white in the blackout'. His coat was collie in type, very glossy and not too luxuriant. But what I liked best was the soft fuzz of whisker on his muzzle and the suggestion of eyebrow in honour of his wire-haired father. His tail was long and bushy, and tapped his sides as he trotted in time with his step, left right, left right.

He was not named for any Australian connections – I don't really have any. No, when I was a child swearing was not allowed; so, having a temper, my devious brain invented my own swear word which would not be recognised as such by the adults in my life. It was diggaluggamunka, a most satisfactory imprecation. I bestowed it on him as his full or formal name, but probably more as an unconscious comment on the war in general. He was only known as Digger for short.

Digger was in many ways a dear little dog, but he had had a very bad start in life and we were both to pay for it. One day when my baby was a few months old I was coming back from an overnight visit to a friend. It was a long way, but I have always enjoyed walking, and swung along happily, pushing the pram with Digger trotting on ahead. But as we got to the corner of our road he suddenly began to scream and tore off to disappear through our garden gate.

As I got there my neighbour came out looking bewildered. Digger had taken refuge in her air raid shelter. This was the first fit he had, but not, alas, the last. The vet told me that he had had repressed distemper, a form in which the dog apparently remains in good health while the illness lasts, but which causes serious and prolonged after effects. Digger's kidneys were damaged and he had nervous lesions which often caused his back legs to fail momentarily so that he fell down, although he always got up again immediately and continued on his way, wagging his tail as ever but with an 'oh dear I am a silly dog' expression on his face which I found infinitely pathetic.

Digger's nerves were very bad, and his reactions like lightning. He was a great one for yelling before he was hurt – he had a scream like a whistling kettle. This could be most embarrassing on occasions. Once he ran after two ladies who often walked past our house with a French bulldog bitch which was the treasure of their hearts. I called and called, whistled and whistled, and was sufficiently annoyed by the time he came back to aim a cuff at him. It didn't land of course – it never did, his reactions were far too quick for that. But that didn't stop him giving tongue with a screech like the damned. The Frenchie's two owners stopped, they turned, they glared, they conferred. To my relief they decided not to come back – no doubt out of concern for Frenchie in case I went indiscriminately berserk – and they never walked past my gate again.

With his senses so acute Digger was a wonderful housedog. He used to lie in the sun on the doorstep beside my baby's pram, and was continually going off like a fire alarm at every passer-by, beginning his protest at the very top of his register. I found this habit most nerve-racking, yet strange to say, he never woke the baby. It must have been all one with the singing of the birds to her although she was a notoriously light sleeper.

We had an elderly Wesleyan deaconess living next door, and I apologised to her for the annoyance caused, explaining that I didn't like to keep the dog in as he was a safeguard against cats getting into the baby's pram. But she said that so far from finding him an annoyance she was pleased to have him there. Being unable to keep a dog herself she felt that he guarded her as well as me and made her feel safe as she lived alone.

Dear Sister Susie! She was truly one of Nature's innocents in spite of the fact that she had been the eldest of a large Irish family. 'We were four girls', she said, 'and then there were four boys and then my mother finished up with two girls and then two more boys to even it up.'

Not surprisingly, she had had to help her mother out by looking after her brothers and sisters, and used to describe to me how she would take the current baby into her bed for warmth and feed it with milk from a fearful contrivance consisting of a bottle with a teat on the end of a long rubber tube. This often leaked, and she and the baby would wake up, both cold and wet through.

Probably all this helped to induce a satiety of family life and contributed to her choice of the church for her career. I don't remember that I ever knew her surname. She was Sister Susie to everybody, and much loved all over what was a pretty mixed district.

The good neighbour who helped to feed Digger, and who lived on the other side of Sister Susie, was very tickled once when Sister Susie told her that she had been out with her collecting box, and, greatly daring, had been into one of the local factories. 'I don't know what they make there,' she said, 'but it's that pretty, clean-looking one on the by-pass.' She had been shown into the manager's office, and on making her appeal was over-joyed to be given a five pound note, which was real money in those days.

'The manager was such a nice man,' she said, 'and he had such a lovely smile.' The joke? She was collecting for the Waifs and Strays and had wandered into a contracep-tive factory! In those bleak wartime days we reckoned the manager had a laugh well worth a fiver, but my neighbour and I were very pleased that he had treated this stray lamb so kindly.

My house was a sort of buffer state between Sister Susie's and my other next door's, who were one of the district's problem families. The good lady there once stole my washing off the line. I felt sorry for her, however, for her husband was a nasty bit of work, said to be both filthy in his habits and violent. I don't know why he wasn't in the forces, but they hadn't missed much. He presumably had a Christian name, but he was known to everyone as Pincher, which I suppose says it all. His wife was a lot like Ma Kettle and I think genuinely loved her brood of young savages in her own way.

27

One day I heard shrieks and howls from her garden, and on looking out saw that they came from the little girl, who was holding a fairly substantial piece of planking, while the eldest boy was threatening her with an enormous saw. There was a crash as the window opened, and the tableau broke up to a roar from Ma – 'Look arter yourself Emmie – 'it 'im on the 'ead wiv it – don't just stand there 'oldin' it!'

So all in all I had quite an interesting war. We were in the flight path from the Continent, which made the nights fairly lively, although this was after the blitz. Owing to Digger's kidney trouble I had had difficulty in housetraining him and never liked to ignore his requests to be let out. But on those bright moonlit nights it was nerve-racking. The garden was only fenced in places, and of course it was impossible to obtain fencing at that time. This didn't matter by day as Digger didn't roam and traffic was limited to the milk float once a day.

But by night it was different. It may have been a hunting instinct aroused by the Hunter's Moon. It may have been Romance, although Romance appeared to lose its allure by day. Perhaps Digger just had a vampire streak in him, but the whole thing was just becoming too much for me. To stand shivering on the doorstep frantically whistling while only too aware of wakeful neighbours cursing me for disturbing what sleep the sirens allowed them, was not my choice at all. Also I was pregnant again, and my baby daughter didn't sleep any more soundly in her cot that she did in her pram.

Still – could I go to bed while my dog was roaming in a moonlight which might explode at any minute into flames? No, I couldn't. Somewhat belatedly I got my brains to work. Next night when Digger raised the 'I gotta go' he found himself outside, but moored securely to a long rope. I went back to bed. In half an hour an indignant yip demanded re-entry. By the end of the week he was cured, to the relief of the whole street. I took it very kindly that no one had actually complained, but I did get one slightly sour note from my kind neighbour. She had been waiting in eager anticipation for her baby's first word.

Would it be Mummy? Would it be Dad-dad? It was neither – it was Digger!

Normally Digger was a very well-behaved little dog and very little trouble apart from his physical weaknesses. These were bad enough. He insisted on sleeping under my bed directly beneath my head, and I don't recommend to anyone the experience of being awakened in the middle of the night by the shrieks of a small dog having a fit about twelve inches from one's ear. Hauled out from beneath the bed on these occasions he would immediately make for the chimney and try to climb up it. I used to have to sponge the base of his skull with cold water to bring him to his senses, after which he would be a very woebegone little chap, cold, shivery, and frightened of his own shadow.

Although we lived in 'bomb alley' we were fairly lucky in that respect. The doodlebugs were the worst, but we had installed a Morrison shelter, which to the uninitiated is a large steel table covering a rudimentary bedspring, enclosed by steel mesh panels and strong enough to support the weight of a collapsing house. My parents also had one and tried to get Scamp to go into it with them during air raids. But poor Scamp was afraid of the creaking springs made of overlapping steel laths, and would only put his head under, so they pulled the heavy dining table alongside and made him a bed there, where he slept with his head under the adjoining shelter.

One doodlebug fell close enough to us to break windows and bring ceilings down, and I once had to snatch my baby from her pram and dive for the gutter when a doodlebug engine cut out and it began hurtling straight for us. Luckily it was one of the newfangled ones with a mechanism which made it change course during its fall. I believe this gadget was meant to increase the terror of the weapon, but in this case it was a very good thing because in changing direction it fell on to some allotments instead of the houses it originally pointed at and so no one was hurt.

Oddly enough one of my worst nights in this period was one – again brightly moonlit – when no bombs fell near although the air raid sirens and anti-aircraft barrage kept me in the Morrison all night. The baby slept sweetly, but Digger, who had had a fit, was pressed hard against my back shivering violently all night. Worst of all my little cat Doreen, hardly more than a kitten, caught a mouse around midnight which must have taken till four o'clock to die. Doreen had so much fun with that unlucky mouse. I could see her agile silhouette outlined in moonlight, coming and going in a macabre ballet. It was like one of the more horrifying sequences from a Disney film. I was unable to rescue the mouse because of the blackout, and in any case I question the mercy of rescue when the victim is probably irremediably damaged. After all, I was alone, and definitely incapable of administering the mouse's quietus if it had been necessary. I just wanted Doreen to finish the poor little beast off quickly and let me get some sleep.

Digger's repressed distemper left him with one strange idiosyncracy, he could not bear to be groomed. I don't mean that he hated it or became vicious. He just couldn't stand it. I think that his skin must have been terribly sensitive, probably due to his general nervous condition, and I realised early on that to persist on this point might bring on a fit. But the strange, and I think I may say wonderful, result, was that he learned to groom himself. He was the only dog I have ever had who really cleaned himself like a cat. He would actually lick his paws and clean behind his ears, and thanks to this and to a distinct fastidiousness which he developed as he matured, I never saw him look otherwise than immaculate once he had acquired his mature adult coat. He never had any skin trouble, and since, thanks to his moderate appetite he was always a neat little figure, he invariably looked in the pink of condition in spite of his poor health.

Poor little Digger. I remember how he hated wet and windy weather. On those days when the wind seemed to pick up the house and give it a shake before blowing right throught it, he would crouch in a corner, with all his hair spiky and on end, his eyes glazed, trembling and uttering a continuous low growl. He occasionally used to do this at other times too, and then we used to say he was seeing ghosts.

We began to wonder if he was seeing fairies too, when we began to find him at the bottom of the garden all alone and apparently practising arabesques and entrechats in the dusky summer twilight. It took us several days to discover that he was actually trying to catch the moths that gathered there: which were those exquisite little creatures apparently made entirely of transparent silver feathers. I believe they are called goat moths, an insultingly inappropriate name which certainly can't derive from their appearance. To look at they were much more like the fairies, so perhaps Digger was misled into believing that was what they really were.

When I took him to see my parents my generous old Scamp received him kindly, and Digger soon had a hero-worship for the old warrior. Like all cowards he was much bullied by his peers, and so tended to keep out of their way. It amused me very much to see the change in him when out for a walk with Scamp. He would approach the nastiest looking dogs brashly, in fact cockily, practically soliciting hostilities. These usually being offered pretty readily he would then skip back to Scamp, whereon the aggressor would at once realise his mistake and quickly and unobtrusively slip out of sight. Scamp at this time was old and lame, and his sight was failing, but there was still that about him that compelled respect.

At the close of the war I felt that at last I could realise my ambition to become a dog breeder. In spite of his many charms Digger had cured me of wanting mongrels. I realised that some at least of his drawbacks were due to his impoverished puppyhood, and saw that a good start in life is one important item justifying the higher price of a well-bred puppy. Good feeding and good care of both bitch and pups lays a strong constitution for the future dog, and both cost money.

When the war ended it seemed as if everyone in England wanted a pedigree dog, as if that was a symbol of the better life we had been promising ourselves. Breeds were changing too, old favourites which had been neglec-

31

ted because of the war were now often forgotten. Airedales were one of these. Instead there began a steady trickle of 'new' foreign breeds, each loudly acclaimed in the dog press as superlative in its field. Some of these, like the boxer (virtually unknown here before 1945) proved to be genuinely individual and valuable additions to our collection of breeds. Others in my opinion were vastly overrated or at least no improvement on the similar native breeds they were superseding.

Fashion is a fickle jade. The day of the poodle was not yet. What the masses fell for, and I was among them, was the cocker spaniel. I had long admired this breed's strong sturdy outline and gentle nature. A head study of a beautiful cocker with its long ears sent shivers down my spine, and I read all I could find about 'the merry cocker'. I thought this a fine title – I still do, but unfortunately in these days it is no longer a true description of so many cockers.

However, my cocker was merry. She was also gentle. She would have been a superlative gun dog, for she was immensely strong and quite tireless. If she thought there was anything in the heart of a bramble patch she went straight in like a tank, energy and keenness alike unflagging. She was also very beautiful, with a true golden cocker coat, feathered and satiny and needing hardly any trimming.

Digger had not had any fits for some time and he and Jane got on famously. It amused me to take them through the woods together and note the difference when they got home. Digger would be immaculate, the very soles of his feet seemed both clean and dry. Jane, on the other hand, always looked as if she had swum through a duckpond and then rolled in the deep ruts. Her paws seemed designed to throw mud all over her golden coat as she ran and she certainly didn't look the aristocrat of the two.

As Digger got older his fits returned and he became very timid. At last there was nothing for it but the last sad trip to the vet's, and the closing of a chapter. He was seven, an age it hadn't seemed likely he would ever reach when he was young. At one time I remember I actually took him to the vet's to have him put down. It was one of his good days and he stood on the table, pretty, glossy and with waving tail. No wonder the vet asked if I really wanted him to go. Of course I didn't, and he told me to give him one more chance. The one more chance was a course of arsenic and strychnine pills – a desperate-sounding remedy enough, but wonder of wonders, they did the trick and gave him those last five years of happy life. So I felt I hadn't done too badly by him. He was my little wartime dog, always happy, patient and undemanding through that difficult time.

What with the air raids, his health problems and my own preoccupation with two small children, I'd never done much in the way of training him. As I've said, he was a naturally well-behaved dog. But I was resolved it should be different with Jane, she really was going to be a superdog.

Unfortunately Jane wasn't listening. Energetic and eager, she went bustling on her way, delighting my eye and trying my patience. I did teach her to stop on the edge of the kerb when I bellowed 'Wait!' She would be dancing with impatience and yelping with excitement until she got the release command 'Over!' when she would shoot across the road. This was quite impressive as she was obviously mad to go on, but what bothered me was the fact that she obviously hadn't the slightest idea why she was waiting and would have unhesitatingly shot under a bus or anything else if I had just given her the word.

Of all my dogs Jane had by far the keenest nose. Airedales have very good scenting powers – the Japanese consider them superior to either Alsatians or Dobermanns in this respect – but I think Jane's talents in this respect would have been outstanding in any breed. You could whip up a pebble from a stony beach and throw it. She would rush over and accept no substitutes till she had the very pebble which your fingers had so fleetingly touched – she was never wrong even if it had landed on a heap of seaweed or decaying fish.

She was a dreadfully greedy dog and an incorrigible

scrounger. She taught me that the hedges and ditches of England are full of fish and chips. We never took a walk where I didn't have to prise some decaying morsel from her clenched jaws. Once she was scampering in her usual don't-stop-me-I'm-busy fashion ahead of me on the pavement when she did an abrupt right turn, whisked over a garden wall and out again with an ancient bone in her mouth before I had even reached the spot.

We called her Vacuum Cleaner from her manner of making her food disappear by placing her head over her dish, and taking a deep breath. At least, that's what it looked like, and she certainly only took a matter of seconds to clear her plate. She was the type of cocker that is very prone to put on fat, and at last I had to ration her to six meals a week. Oddly she never worried for food on her fast day. Even this didn't make her slim, but it did keep her fast and light on her feet. It sounds an awful thing to do but I believe it used to be (and still is) a common practice in some kennels and was thought to keep the dogs healthy. I'm glad I've never had to do it since, but when I see some of the ton-weight cockers struggling around, all of whose owners will assure you that 'he doesn't eat much' it seems a pity it isn't more often done now.

Scamp died, fourteen years exactly to the day since we first had him as a five-week old baby. Although it was years since I had left him in my parents' house I felt a gap. He had been my thirteenth birthday present. I had left school, gone to work, married, had two children and lived through a war in his lifetime. He was also a link with my sister Nell who had been killed when a bomb hit her house. She had been Scamp's best beloved, and although she had been married and living away from us when it happened, Scamp knew, and I think he was never the same dog again, even though he still had much of his life to live. He had given both of us great joy and taught me many things. I was a different person for having known him, and now he was gone.

Jane was still young, but I didn't seem to have made much headway with her training. Especially when I remembered the three-figure list of commands and words I had made for Scamp when no older than she was. Jane, as I have said, just wasn't listening. Happy and preoccupied, she bustled on her way with a swish of her skirts and her ears like two great golden chrysanthemums flying about her satin neck. Regretfully I had to accept that the direct communication I had taken for granted with Scamp would never exist between me and Jane. It was as if there were a glass wall between us. Even her pleasure in a caress was only too obviously her pleasure in an enjoyable physical sensation, not in an expression of love.

I don't wish to be unfair to Jane, because she was really all a cocker should be – merry, gentle, sweet tempered. She did not steal, she was not destructive, she was clean and she was quiet. She was always a joy to the eye and in her limited way quite obedient. I have since seen cockers work very well in Obedience trials so I know they are not all tone deaf to commands; nevertheless Jane cured me of cockers much as Digger had cured me of mongrels.

Having said all this, however, there remained the positive side of Jane's account. She was in many ways my first. My first pedigree puppy – in fact the first time I ever went personally to pick a puppy for myself from a litter – my first bitch, my first showdog. And my first litter of puppies was bred from her. So she was very important in my life.

The very first show I ever attended, I entered Jane and she won a first. This should have been enought to set me alight on a doggy career, but sad to say showing was very difficult for me because of domestic reasons. I only showed her once more, and got, as far as I can remember, a third. However, my real interest lay in breeding and I knew everything the books could tell me. Unfortunately there were quite a lot of things they didn't tell me.

As Jane's first birthday drew near I examined her daily for signs of heat. Just as well I did, because although the books said this began with a straw-coloured discharge followed by a bloodstained one, Jane's never progressed beyond the straw stage. In fact she was one of those bitches, fairly rare but by no means unknown, who never do 'show colour'.

In Jane's case at least this didn't seem to affect her fertility and she went on to produce two litters. I will deal with them in more detail later on.

Although I was anxious to become a breeder I intended to use Jane also to further my children's education. They had already grasped the difference between pedigree dogs and mongrels. I explained that Jane's long ears and short tail were the result of her being a cocker spaniel and a pedigree dog. I was amused by my little son's interest in this information but not prepared for his dismissing a handsome bullmastiff as a mongrel because 'He's got short ears and a long tail.' The bullmastiff's owner was *not* amused.

It's not long since my son's own little son told his mother that he was going to have a puppy of his own when he was bigger. She asked him what kind of puppy he was going to have, and he replied firmly 'A puppy on a lead.'

Jane's seasons could not be tactfully ignored because of the risk of the children leaving doors open during these crucial periods, so I told him that there were times when Janie was ready to make babies, and that this could only be done by her playing with a boy dog. I explained the need for care with the doors by telling him that the puppies would be mongrels unless the boy dog was also a cocker spaniel.

Stephen was fascinated by this information. Once he had grasped the idea that the babies would look like both parents he amused himself by imagining what they would be like should she play with, say, an Alsatian – they would have Janie's ears, he decided, but they would stand right up like an Alsatian's! The imagination boggles, but he thought he had me when he asked, with an expression of great cunning, 'What sort of puppies will Janie have if she plays with a *bitch*?'

As he was so keen on the dogs I promised him a puppy out of Janie's second litter. There was a very beautiful bitch puppy there which should have been ideal, but unfortunately we were then living in a council flat and the council vetoed it so that was that. The official who brought these glad tidings said that Stephen might keep a rabbit *provided I first submitted plans of the rabbit hutch.* I didn't bother.

Stephen, then five, had been much involved with this litter, pacing the floor outside Jane's lying-in room like any prospective father. After the whelping I strictly forbade him to touch the puppies unless I was there. Imagine my horror on the following day to find him actually sitting in the box and carefully holding a whelp up for Jane to clean its bottom, which she was doing.

I had him out as fast as possible compatible with not being too sudden and alarming the bitch. To my recriminations he merely replied 'But I was *helping* Janie to look after her puppies and she liked it!' Looking back I'm not sure she didn't; at any rate she showed no resentment, only a serious absorption in the job in hand. As I said, she was all a cocker is supposed to be in gentleness. Even so there must be very few bitches of any breed who would allow this sort of thing from so young an assistant just after the birth of their babies.

I sold the bitch puppy for about two-thirds of her real value; but the two dog pups I practically gave away, things were so difficult at that time. I did have an offer from a wholesaler which I am happy to say I refused. These were very fine puppies in every way and inherited Jane's gentle nature. The bitch and one of the dogs I consider were championship standard and I think better than any of Jane's first family of seven, all of whom had sold well. This is the sort of thing that makes dog breeding such a gamble. If you intend to keep a puppy and eagerly look forward to the litter you will probably find it does not contain a pup suitable for your purpose. But if a super puppy arrives unlooked for, it is usually at a time when for some reason you can't keep it.

Jane was only five when she died. She picked up an infection which got into her bloodstream. Penicillin was then only newly available for animal medicine. My vet gave her as much as she dared, but it wasn't quite enough. The infection was almost cured but not quite, and before long she was suffering so much that the end was inevitable.

Luckily the children were at the sea with relatives when she took her last sad journey to the vet. This saved them the worst moment, and although they were a little upset when they came home and we told them, they were still very young and so full of their seaside adventures that the edge of our bad news was considerably dulled.

We didn't believe in telling them fairy stories to account for her disappearance. I have a feeling that the 'lovely home in the country' so beloved of romantics would have gone down badly. How can any child who loves a dog accept the thought that his parents have given it to someone else? Especially a dog like Jane, who had always done her best and been a totally unobjectionable member of the family?

Besides, it is one of the most valid reasons for keeping a dog with children that they can learn from it many of the facts of life. Jane had already taught mine as many of the facts of birth as they were capable of grasping; now she taught them the fact of death. They knew that she had been ill and had been going to the vet, and they accepted our explanation that the vet had been unable to cure her and that she had been given a merciful release from pain. Some people criticised us for doing it while the children were away, behind their backs, as it were, but I believe we were right. When I remember the really bitter agony I experienced in my own childhood on such occasions, and then the momentary check in the tale of seaside wonders which was the only immediate reaction to the news, I know we were right.

As I say, they were both very young, and I expect another five or eight years might have brought a very different response. They did miss her and they did talk about her afterwards with affection and regret, but the initial shock was virtually avoided altogether.

And myself? To be honest I suffered so much in anticipation, for I had known for some weeks that she must die, that the end in itself came almost as a relief. Strange to say Jane never looked more beautiful than in her last weeks, probably because she was losing weight and in consequence had her best figure ever. She was a real eyecatcher, and continually drew remarks from all who saw her – admirers who had no idea that she had only a week or two more to live. Their compliments were really more than I could bear, and some kind people must have thought me very odd indeed as I couldn't look them in the eye but got away as fast as I could for fear of disgracing myself.

4

Bamu

Long before we lost Jane I had made up my mind that there could be only one dog for me next time. I was having perhaps more than my share of troubles and my health was very bad indeed. The world often seemed a chill and inhospitable place, and my pleasure in my children often paled in the conviction that they'd drawn the short straw when they picked their Mum.

The non-doggy may snort with disgust if they like, but in this miserable, confused period one of the things I remember best is the sudden agonising lurch of the heart I felt whenever I saw, or thought I saw, an Airedale. One bleak January morning I wandered into Woolworth's, where they were clearing out the bent and battered remains of their Christmas stock, and came face to face with a marvellous picture of an Airedale, peering smiling round the edge of an open door.

It was a sepia photograph, not in mint condition, and the little calendar which should have hung from it was missing. Believe it or not, I had to walk round all the other counters before I could control my face and voice enough to ask the assistant for it. To my dismay she worried about it having no calendar attached and wanted to go through the box to find one, any one, that was complete. Convincing her that I did in fact want that picture and no other was one of the most difficult things I have ever done as I could hardly speak. I had that picture for years and wish I still had it, it was such a comfort to me, but it was probably ditched by some kind relative during one of the many times we moved house.

So after Janie's demise I announced that our next dog was going to be an Airedale. The children took this very well considering that they hadn't much idea of what an Airedale was like, neither of them really remembering Scamp.

When it came to implementing my decision I came up against two difficulties. One was money – I hadn't any. However, my little boy and I both had birthdays coming up, so I suggested to him that we both ask for our gifts in cash this time, then pool the result and buy an Airedale as our joint property. He agreed enthusiastically.

The second difficulty oddly enough I didn't realise existed, and in the event it never came up. If this sounds double Dutch let me explain. The fact was that the breed was very scarce in this country at that time. Later I often met people who told me that they had hunted for years for an Airedale puppy and eventually been forced to settle for another breed.

This might well have been my fate but for that guardian angel who has been so helpful in times of crisis. The very first local paper that I bought, the very weekend that Stephen and I had pooled our modest fortunes, carried an advertisement for Airedale puppies 'cheap to good homes'. It may well have been the only one in ten years.

Rushing to the nearest phone box I rang the number given. The man answering said that the puppies had actually been bred by his brother in Bury St Edmunds. He was bringing some puppies from there at the weekend and they would be available on Monday. I told him to be sure and bring some bitches, took the address and went home to get through the weekend as best I could.

Well, I think that Monday was one of the most important days in my life, a turning point in fact, so it is not surprising that I remember it all so clearly. Having no car I had to travel first on a bus and then on a tram, and literally shivered with excitement and anticipation all the way there. The tram stopped a few yards from the house I wanted, and outside the house itself a gang of workmen were digging up the road with pneumatic drills.

It was a tall, dingy, depressing-looking house and the door was opened by a tall, dingy, depressing-looking man. When I mentioned puppies he invited me in and I followed him down a long dark passage covered only with badly worn linoleum and into a large uncarpeted room with precious little furniture in it and in urgent need of redecoration. The whole atmosphere was quite Dickensian.

I reminded the man that I wanted a bitch, and he asked me to wait while he fetched them from the garage. In speaking of puppies I was thinking of something small and cuddly, like the litter of spaniels from which I had picked Jane; but I soon heard a rush of scampering feet, and in bounded two leggy puppies considerably more advanced than that.

As they quietened down I saw that one was rather small, with runny eyes, and ran mostly on three legs, only putting the fourth foot down now and then. The other, which was sound, looked much bigger and stronger all round. I had hoped for a big one, and had enough sense to know I shouldn't buy trouble, so I told the man I would take the larger of the two. She was obviously too big for me to carry all the way home, so I asked him if he had anything I could use as a lead. In the meantime the little one had run off with my gloves. I rescued them and began to read the pedigree, but she had them again. Catching her this time I saw how beautiful her eyes were. Even if they were runny they were much darker than her sturdy sister's. In fact the larger puppy looked quite plain beside her.

42

I went back to the pedigree and tried to concentrate on it when suddenly I heard a voice say quite plainly in my ear, 'You're taking home the wrong dog.' Thinking it over I'm inclined to believe it must have been that Guardian Angel again, the only time he has directly addressed me in all our long association. If so, thank you Guardian Angel, I never had better advice in my life.

When the man came in again I told him that I had changed my mind and would take the smaller puppy. His immediate reaction – 'The price is the same.' What did I care? He had brought me an old belt to use as combined collar and lead, and said that as the puppy was fresh up from the country and would be frightened by the noise of the drills outside he would carry her to the tram for me. Kind, I thought, and we were soon aboard, clanging and swaying on our way.

But when I got off the tram to change to the bus I discovered the reason for his solicitude – the puppy had an alarming-looking knob protruding from her tummy. I felt a bit dashed but decided not to panic until the vet had seen her. Skinny little thing with a gammy leg and runny eyes, riddled with worms, and as it transpired, running alive with fleas and lice. And now with a mysterious lump in her middle. It didn't matter. I knew with complete certainty that this was the dog for me, and from the first moment that I took her into my arms she filled me with a warmth and gladness that were like a breath of life to me. A premonition perhaps, because she was without doubt the most important purchase I ever made in my life.

Poor little Bamu. Bewildered but trusting, she had yet another ordeal ahead of her that day. We had a cat at home which had been very good friends with Jane. Technically just an alley cat he was yet an exceptionally beautiful one, a short-haired mackerel tabby. Three raven-black stripes ran from the tip of his nose, over his head, down his neck and back to the very end of his restless tail. His main colour was a true silver grey, shading to powder blue on his soft undercarriage. He had no other stripes, but his body was exquisitely marked with lines of raven black spots, and when I say raven black I mean it, for his markings shone purple and green in the sunlight just as the plumage of a raven does.

Before leaving home that morning I had taken the precaution of shutting Puddy in the sitting-room. I didn't want him walking in completely ignorant that a new dog had been added to the strength. I thought that if he saw the puppy he would arch his back and retire to the garden to think it over, then return to spy out the land and get acquainted. I was quite unprepared for what actually happened. Picking up my new treasure and saying softly, 'Look, Pud, see what I've got,' I stepped into the room.

Puddy was sitting bolt upright on the floor directly opposite me. To my amazement he spat like a siphon and launched himself in one great arc across the room at my chest. There was a piercing yelp from the puppy and Puddy was out of the door and up the garden. He had torn her eye, so there was I with my sorry specimen looking sorrier than ever, waiting for the vet – and none of the family had even seen her yet.

I had better recount here what the man had told me. First he said the puppies were three months old and had been bred by his brother who was giving up because they had had so much illness. When I asked what diseases he replied vaguely, 'Oh everything' and refused to be more specific. My little one, he said, had been very bad; in fact they had not expected her to recover. Moreover she had injured her leg trying to get out of the pen – the fence had fallen on it. All this had disenchanted his brother with the idea of breeding dogs. He had decided to cut his losses and go in for pigs instead, hence the low prices. Yes, I paid three guineas for Bamu. The price at that time was about eight, so she really was cheap – if she lived.

For my vet, when she arrived, took a gloomy view. The animation which had given Bamu that sparkle and made her steal my gloves was all gone. Instead she saw a woebegone, bony runt with but three sound legs and barely enough strength to stand on those. She had known me for a long time and asked if I had paid much for the dog. I said no, she was advertised as cheap to a good home, whereon she sniffed and said it was as well she *had*

44

come to a good home because she obviously hadn't had much luck so far. Jealous for my new darling I said defensively that she obviously badly needed worming and would be better when that was done, and was somewhat startled to get the reply, 'You'll kill this dog if you worm her. I doubt if you'll rear her in any case.'

However, she said that Pud's claws had only penetrated the cornea and that only in the extreme corner of the eye, so it should heal up all right. It did. The other runniness wasn't important, probably mostly weakness, and to my great relief, that lump in her tummy was just an umbilical hernia and nothing to worry about as it contained nothing but a little fat.

She was more concerned about the leg. She thought the puppy had a torn ligament and that the two centre toes, which pointed heavenward, would never come right. She disbelieved the man's story; she thought Bamu had either been struck by a car or hit with a stick. However in all fairness I will say that I think he told the truth. Bamu was always afraid of walking near board fences and was also nervous of the sound of wood against wood, for example the noise of my gateleg table being extended or put away.

My vet gave me another shock when she examined her teeth. 'Three months? This dog'll never see six months again, she's got all her teeth.' Re-examination of the pedigree revealed that Bamu was in fact eight months old! She was no larger than a fox terrier. So much for my ambition to own a really big one.

Through all this that feeling of warmth never wavered. Bamu soon proved to have very little stamina – a little burst of gaiety and animation followed by near collapse was the pattern. No doubt this was a convalescent condition aggravated by the leg injury. As it happened my own condition wasn't much better, so we made a good pair. I very much enjoyed nursing Bamu, feeding her lots of small meals packed with proteins, vitamins and minerals, and increasing her strength with frequent short walks and games played in the house.

And she bloomed. In a matter of days she was on all four legs, the toes came right down to meet the ground, and not only was her movement entirely unaffected, but even in old age she never showed any signs of rheumatism or arthritis as is usual in an injured limb. Her eyes cleared up as her health improved. Cleared of all parasites she put on flesh and actually grew three inches in her first two weeks with us. She had the very best sort of Airedale coat, hard and thick and dirt-resistant, with the richest colouring and plenty of whisker and leg hair.

But best of all was her character. Bamu was a perfect example of what Paul Jennings once called 'one of these dog saints'. In our family we have another name for them. We call such a dog a 'one in a million', and there is absolutely no means known to man to ensure either the production or acquisition of them. They pop up disguised as fat little mongrels or Crufts winners, rich or poor, beloved or persecuted. Bamu became the ancestress of all my Airedales since that day, and of many, many more, and while they certainly proved strong in good temperament I couldn't swear that any of them has been her equal in saintliness, although there may have been some among the puppies I have sold and lost track of.

About her name, by the way, I always tell people that it is an African name meaning 'too good and too beautiful', but this isn't really true. I actually got it from Joyce Carey's book 'Mister Johnson'. Bamu was the name of the tribal beauty whom Mr Johnson married. In the book I fear Bamu was by no means an admirable character, being lazy, selfish, faithless and stupid, but her husband thought she was perfect and invariably referred to her as 'that too good beautiful Bamu', hence the name.

I'm happy to say that my Bamu was quite different, gentle, loving, gay, keenly intelligent and anxious to please. By bedtime on the first day she knew her name, and by the end of the first week she knew those of all the family. Puddy soon fell under her spell and she adored the children, who were delighted with her playfulness.

She was a boon to them on wet days. They would sit one at each end of the hall, having first taken up the rugs, and roll or bounce a ball to each other – throwing was strictly forbidden as the ball had to be kept low to avoid damage.

Bamu was piggy in the middle, and it took skilful play to get the ball past her. She got her share of the ball and a lot of kissing and cuddling when they got it from her again. This game was called Blackberry Polo – the blackberry being the black knob on the end of Bamu's nose.

Towards the end of her first summer she joined in family cricket as fielder, always taking the ball back to the bowler. The vet, seeing her six months after that first ominous day, couldn't believe it was the same dog.

She loved to fetch things. Like Scamp she learned the names of a lot of articles. I have often stood at the French windows at the end of a summer's day and asked her to fetch in from the garden the various bits of clothing, and toys, discarded by the children now in bed. She was very pleased and proud to do this because she was heart and soul my dog, never at ease unless I was around.

I remember being out with her when she was just beginning to gain some strength, and meeting an acquaintance who, in deference to my corpse-like aspect, urged me to 'get rid of that great bouncy dog – you can always get another when you're better.' Get rid of her! She was my lifeline. She had kindled a warmth in me on that first journey home which never failed me. But how awful if I hadn't been my own mistress – if some well-meaning guardian had taken this well-wisher's advice – it would have just about finished me to have lost Bamu at that point in my life.

Bamu was so gentle and sweet to everyone that it never occurred to me to think of her as a guard dog. One Christmas Eve she and I were alone in our rather isolated house when a tramp came to the door selling white heather. He wouldn't take no for an answer, and I was just beginning to feel a little uneasy as he began looking behind me to the empty stairs and kitchen. Bamu was eating dog-biscuits in the hall just behind me, and I really didn't give her a thought. Whether she caught my anxiety, or whether the tramp's voice had really taken on a more menacing note I can't say, but she suddenly erupted like a volcano, and not satisfied with making terrible threatening noises she made a rush for him. I just caught her as she tried to shoot past me, and the tramp was out of the gate like greased lightning, mumbling furiously 'I didn't know you had a dog!'

This is part of the Airedale nature, so friendly and outgoing with one and all that many people entirely discount them as guards, yet seeming to know when strong measures are called for. As far away as Japan they are valued for this property because apparently they don't make mistakes between the goodies and the baddies!

Bamu showed her concern for me another time when I had my head stuck out of the window talking to a neighbour. She suddenly began crying and pawing at my legs. When I looked round I found that she was so distressed because a saucepan on the stove beside me was boiling over and forming a soapy pool round my feet. She probably thought I was in danger of drowning!

About a year after I bought her we moved into a new house with a big garden, and I was able to look forward to breeding my first litter of Airedales. My little substandard bag of shivering bones had blossomed into a dancing bundle of fun and personality, and I now often had the satisfaction of being envied by the very people who had looked down their noses at her before.

Bamu had a reasonably good pedigree containing the names of two of the most important dogs of the day, namely Wyrewood Apollo and Solo Aristocrat. She was an outcross – that is, there was little connection between the sire's and dam's side of her pedigree. If I were mating her today I would try to find a dog carrying some of this good blood in his own pedigree: then I could expect to get a fairly even litter which would be an improvement, as far as show points go, on their mother.

But Airedales, as I have pointed out, were very thin on the ground in those days; in fact people often actually asked what breed Bamu was. Also I wasn't in touch with the showing fraternity, so when I made the acquaintance of a very handsome dog within convenient reach I didn't hesitate. My own ambition was to have a daughter of Bamu's who would be just like her so that I could look forward to an unfailing supply of Bamus for the rest of my life.

48

Don was a very fine dog with a superb head and front, which is dog-ese for the front view of a dog, meaning his neck, legs and chest. In an Airedale this is supposed to be straight and narrow, giving much the same impression as a double-barrelled gun, hence the expression 'gun-barrel front'. We had a little trouble getting them mated. Don was keen but a bit confused as to procedure, but fortunately Bamu was all for the proposed union and flirted shamelessly till it was consummated.

We put up a big makeshift box in a corner of the sitting-room, and there Bamu produced her first family, two girls and five boys. The second girl was the last born and the smallest; she also cried the loudest. The runt, I thought, so that only left the other bitch, who was big and strong and always made sure she got the best of what was going in the way of milk. That wasn't much, unfortunately, because Bamu was feverish, wouldn't eat, and was soon unable to nurse her babies.

The vet came and diagnosed an infection. Poor Bamu desperately wanted to look after her puppies, who were all crying now as I hadn't much idea of how to make good her deficiency, but she just couldn't bear them round her. I put her chair next to the box and she not only made a bed in it but found her favourite ball and took that up with her and nursed that instead. This ball, which we called her Tinkerball because it had a hole in it containing a bell, became a substitute baby which she never forgot. I think it would have been cruel to have forced her to nurse the puppies in the state she was in; it might have done a lot of harm, deferred her recovery and possibly made her anti-puppy for life. But I was desperate because she still wouldn't eat, so I baked a batch of chocolate buns and loaded them with soft chocolate icing. Bamu was always an inveterate cakehound and even in her present condition found them irresistible. They kept her going over-night and her milk came back the next day as the medicine took effect and she improved.

Of course there were howls of disappointed rage when the children smelt the chocolate buns on their return from school and were then told they were for the dog! I must say they took it very well when I explained the reason, and were rewarded with one each.

It was a good job that our garden, besides being big, was very much in the rough. Bamu's boys, as we called that litter, rampaged all over it. Like Jane, Bamu was an excellent mother and she loved her babies and knew any one of them instantly even if she had not seen it for some years. One by one they were sold until we were left with only the big bitch puppy which had been formally presented to my daughter Naomi. The little bitch, incidentally, was sold and called Butch, a name she proceeded to live up to by growing as big and strong as her sister, whom she much resembled.

Although our puppy was a bitch among a preponderately male bunch she was obviously the leader of the gang. A fact which might have given us food for thought.

5

T. F. Toffee Nut

Naomi had some difficulty in choosing a name for her puppy so I suggested she thought of something she liked very much. She replied 'Biscuits – or toffee.' And Toffee it was. I had already registered Bamu at the Kennel Club as Bamu of Caterways (the name of our house) and later adopted Caterways as my kennel affix. Before we had settled on an official name for Toffee it so happened that Naomi wrote a long story as a holiday task. It was about a family shipwrecked on an island à la Swiss Family Robinson. The heroines, needless to say, were the young daughter and her intrepid puppy Toffee. While exploring the resources of the island the puppy was found to be eating some delicious nuts which tasted of toffee and so the family gratefully named them Toffee Nuts in her honour.

So when it came to choosing Toffee's name it was there ready. It was already obvious that Toffee was something of a nut, so Toffee Nut she became officially. To this we privately added the initials T.F., standing for The Famous, and had some reason for doing so.

Every one of my dogs as I write about it seems to be 'the most' in some respect. What shall I say about T.F. Toffee Nut? She was just – the most. She was a sort of natural disaster of a dog, like an earthquake or a landslide or tidal wave. She was certainly the most intelligent. She has some competition for that title, but if Bamu was a saint among dogs, Toffee was undeniably a dog genius. Not that it was any use to anybody but herself; Toffee kept her brains strictly for her own personal use.

As far as I could see Toffee only resembled her little mother in one respect: her good temper was completely and utterly unflappable. But, if Bamu was small, Toffee was enormous, the biggest Airedale bitch I have ever seen. She must have been half as big again as her little Mum. Then where Bamu was sensitive and anxious to please, Toffee hadn't a nerve of any sort in her body and couldn't have cared less whether anybody was pleased with her or not.

Toffee was only eleven weeks old when an incident occurred which, if I had but realised it, was a sort of portent of the future. She was supposed to be playing in the garden with Laddie, the last remaining dog puppy, when I realised she was missing. I ran around frantically but she was nowhere to be seen.

Seeing an ice cream van stopped a little way along the street I grabbed Laddie and went and asked the driver if he had seen a puppy just like this one. He hadn't, but a few minutes after driving off he was back with the truant on his knee. He had spotted her heading for the local council estate in company with a gang of children. From this incident she retained a lifelong kindness for small children and ice cream, but most of all for running away. Running away, in fact, became to her what dogs have been to me, an all-absorbing interest and raison d'être.

At the age of four months Toffee went on the stage. It was only a school play, but I was told she was much fêted and a huge success. Possibly this precocious triumph also had its part in turning her head. I don't know. I only know that the tried and trusted methods which I had used with some success since Scamp had been a puppy just weren't working.

And how she grew! She might have been a judgement on me for wanting a big one. Worse still, like Tigger, whatever she weighed in pounds shillings and ounces, she always seemed bigger because of the bounces.

And could she bounce! It was funny out of doors to see how completely she confused would-be fighters by bounding round them in six-foot arcs till they gave up the idea and staggered giddily away. Not so funny indoors when she swooped in from the garden at full gallop and then hurled herself through the serving hatch as the shortest route to her mecca, the kitchen. She thought this was a great joke and obviously expected a round of applause – which she didn't get.

Toffee was a great enthusiast. Everything she did was done with a wholeheartedness at once terrifying and disarming. It was like living with a cross between a horse and a bear, but a bear without malice, and a horse so busy having a good time that it sometimes seemed churlish to cavil at the fact that she was a strain on every resource we possessed.

Toffee was a great enjoyer, and that is a trait which I in turn enjoy. We used to say that even when she was disgruntled she enjoyed her misery. She had a habit of mooing like a cow which was very expressive of her sense of persecution when deprived of any object or course of action which she desired. Most Airedales, incidentally, have their own ways of talking – vocally, I mean. Bamu gave me striking proof of this.

Puddy, who had a passion for cheese, was a thief. He would steal the cheese from the table, but he wouldn't eat it until he had taken it on to the floor. Toffee and Bamu wouldn't steal from the table, but regarded anything on the floor as theirs. So Puddy really hadn't a hope of making crime pay, he was robbed in turn as he hit the carpet and the dogs got a free cheese feast.

But Bamu, as I said, was a saint and knew this wasn't *right*. She therefore decided she had better grass on Pud, and to do it invented a most peculiar remark, something between a howl and a whine. Now this noise meant one thing and one thing only – 'Mum, the cat's on the table!' This is the nearest thing I have ever come across in canine-to-human speech, because she never made this noise for any other reason – it was directly designed to convey specific information. I also consider it a striking proof of Bamu's nobility of soul because she liked cheese as much as anybody else, and by obeying her conscience and sneaking to teacher she was deliberately renouncing the fleshpots for love.

Of course, all this was when Toffee was older, because in her younger days she was an inveterate thief herself. This was something I had virtually no experience of before, and with Toffee's particular type of bulldog mentality found it a daunting task to cure.

First I tried my usual and previously effective method – smacking my hand down viciously on the table beside the intruding nose, accompanied by a forceful 'NO!' Toffee didn't seem to notice this, or possibly she regarded it as a mere cheery greeting, for she was that sort of dog, reading into hostile behaviour whatever meaning best suited her own evil ends at the time. Besides this, most of her thieving was done on the wing, as it were, for with her great height and superb accuracy she could snatch any item of food she fancied without faltering in her stride as she rushed past.

I decided to try cunning. What about the traditional dogman's trick of leaving out a tempting piece of meat spread thick with mustard? Well, putting meat out for Toffee was like shooting peas into a bucket – you could hear it land on the floor of her stomach without touching the sides on the way down. Bread would be better, highly acceptable to our Toff without awakening the ravening wolf that dwelt in her entrails.

A nice thick chunky bit, plastered richly with strongest Colman's was duly placed strategically on the kitchen table, and after leaving the back door ajar I withdrew to keep secret observation through the serving hatch.

In from the garden bounded Toffee, hurling the door

54

aside with her usual crash, spotted the bait and promptly whipped it. It obviously met with her approval. Never at a loss, she first scraped off the mustard on the doormat, ate the bread, went back and carefully licked up the mustard, then came back to the table and put her paws up to see if there was any more going. A success from her point of view if not from mine.

Lying in bed one Sunday morning I heard a crash and didn't hurry down, under the erroneous impression that there was nothing filchable on the table. I found out my mistake half an hour later – Toffee had knocked down a jar of gooseberry jam. All the jam had gone, and on examination, so had half the jar. A sticky situation in every sense.

I fed her part of a large loaf, washed down by vast quantities of water in which the dogs' fish had been boiled. She swelled visibly before our eyes, but this somewhat homespun remedy apparently worked and she suffered no ill effects.

I have since learned that what I should have fed her was cotton wool sandwiches. I'm sure she would have loved them. Apparently the wool encloses the sharp edges and enables them to pass through without injury to the dog.

I kept leaving out less delectable goodies such as raw onions, lemons and used grapefruit rinds, and Toffee's raiding technique did begin to slow a bit. Then I thought of keeping a sort of permanent booby trap of cake tins on the edge of the table. Every time Toffee passed me at the table I could with a flick of my hand bring the lot down round her ears. They didn't hurt her but they did make an awful noise, and this really made her wonder whether the pleasures of the table weren't overrated.

Finally I taught her the good old trick On Trust and Paid For, at which she became very good. So the cure was at last complete. I could even leave the Sunday joint to keep hot in the hearth and know that neither dog would touch it.

But Toffee always had an eye to the main chance. Some years later I took refuge in our local baker's from a sudden cloudburst. People weren't so fussy then about dogs going into food shops and I took mine in with me as a matter of course. There were no other customers, and after buying my loaves I stood chatting with the girl behind the counter while I waited for the storm to blow over.

Suddenly her eyes widened and she cried out, 'Look at your dog!'

That fiend Toffee had been making good use of her time. Standing stock still so as not to pull on the lead and give the game away, she was quietly eating chocolate éclairs out of the window! When the assistant counted, she found that she had had four and was on her fifth! Of course I had to pay for them, but fortunately the girl was highly amused by Toff's discernment. 'She knew which ones to choose,' she said, 'She never bothered with the plain ones, did she?'

It always annoys me when scientists say that dogs don't think and can't reason. I've come across a good many incidents that prove the opposite to me. It's true that these powers cannot be tested in laboratory conditions because one never knows what will trigger such incidents off, and proud owners often misinterpret their pets' mental processes.

A customer who recently told me that she believed her dog to be very stupid, was quite cockahoop on her second visit because his behaviour in the car as they neared my house convinced her that he knew where they were going, so he must be really intelligent after all. I didn't like to dampen her enthusiasm, but to me it was just straight memory accompanied by the appropriate reaction. It neither proved nor disproved the dog's intelligence, but it is this sort of thing that makes the sceptics chary of believing the claims of dog owners in general.

When Toffee was still an outsize puppy I watched her playing in the garden with a marrowbone one day. She was tossing it about and pouncing on it and having a high old time generally. Then she gave it an extra twist, and it sailed over her head and came down in soft earth behind some flowers. She obviously didn't hear it land and was very puzzled because she couldn't see it either, and without leaving that one spot turned round several times,

56

peering anxiously in all directions, an animated question mark. . . .

Here is where a less intelligent dog would have given up or possibly begun barking for help. Not so Toff. No, she obviously reasoned that if the bone wasn't on the ground then it hadn't come down, therefore it must still be up in the air; and to my astonishment she stood up on her hind legs and began slowly revolving with her head on one side searching the sky.

True, this wasn't very bright by our standards, but if she hadn't been mistaken in her first premise, i.e. that the bone wasn't on the ground, would it have been so silly? If it had got caught on some obstruction such as a tree branch she would have been justified. After all, she was still only a puppy and didn't have a lot of experience of falling marrow bones to go on. I have always considered that this was a true train of thought.

Toffee had a lot of off-beat talents. Besides mooing like a cow she was very good at killing wasps. She used to sit in the open French window in summer and snap at them as they flew in from the garden, taking them head on and spitting them out in two halves. She was never stung.

She was also immensely strong, utterly tireless and quite without nerves. These qualities didn't necessarily improve her as a pet. Our wrath and felicitations came alike to her. Paradoxically she was a very loving and warm-hearted dog without an atom of vice, but so long as she was enjoying herself she couldn't have cared less whether she was top of our pops or a candidate for being skinned alive. If you thrashed her – and I'm afraid that in desperation we sometimes did – she seemed to look on it as a minor natural disaster, like a thunderstorm, nicer when it was over, but for which no one need feel guilty or look for causes. She would shake herself cheerfully, and then, with an almost audible 'Now what was I doing before all that?' go on with whatever course of action had provoked your violence. One got a distinct feeling of helplessness sometimes when trying to cope with Toffee.

But far and away the worst thing about her was her passion for running. As far as the recall was concerned she was frankly untrainable. Oh yes, we *taught* her to come and she knew at once what we meant and would even do it if she hadn't anything better on at the time, but we never got to that stage in our relationship when we could call her and *know* that she would obey. This meant that walks ceased to be the pleasant outings they had been when we had Bamu only, and became a series of battles in a long, long war.

When she was small I used to take them to the nearest common and let them off the lead. They would promptly set about each other with a racket of snarling, snapping, scrapping and growling quite terrifying to other walkers who didn't know it was all in fun and usually couldn't see the gladiators anyway because they were deep in bracken. This was both embarrassing and exhausting to me. I have often gone home from these walks tired, miserable, and with legs feeling like jelly and wobbly with it.

I decided that I would take Toffee out by herself in order to train her. There were some very pleasant wide unmade roads near us, and I began to train her there without her lead, although looking back it seems incredible to me that I ever had that much optimism. Toffee treated these roads exactly as if they were the common. After tearing madly back and forth across the road a few times, nose to ground, she suddenly cleared a garden wall and shot round the back of the house.

Here her attention was riveted by a bird-table. It was well within her reach standing on her hind legs and I could see my carefully nurtured pup avidly scoffing the grisly collection of crusts and stale fat put out for our feathered friends. Of course I was calling and whistling like mad, but having cleared the board, instead of returning to me she went on to the next garden. Here was another bird-table which got the same treatment, and all I could do was to follow down the road while she moved on a parallel course fifty yards away, leaping fences and robbing bird-tables with great satisfaction until both ran out at the end of the road. Then another danger became apparent. She decided it would be friendlier to rush back and give me a lick of thanks before giving the other side of the road the same treatment.

It took me three quarters of an hour to catch her. I don't know what the residents thought. I never dared take her down that road again in case someone was lying in wait for her with a gun.

Next I bought a twelve-yard clothes line and tried her down another road with this tied to her collar instead of a lead. At first it looked as if this would be a success. Nobody more surprised than Toff when brought up short in mid-lawn. She soon grasped the principle that she was supposed to walk on the pavement and not leap around the landscape indiscriminately. Preening myself and thinking smugly that it only took a little imagination and perseverance, I decided after a few days of this that the rope could be dispensed with. Happy Toff! Hooray, she thought, free once more, and promptly made tracks for the nearest bird-table scented on the wind.

I remembered Scamp and Jane and the bicycle trick. Travelling at some speed there seemed to be a good chance that Toffee would have no time to deviate. Here I mistakenly made the basic assumption that we would be travelling in the same direction, a thought which obviously didn't occur to her. I only tried it once. It began with one mad wild sortie into a bullock field and ended with me pushing my bike home on quivering legs, with Toffee once more back on the lead.

And there we decided she must remain apart from free runs in open spaces. It seemed a pity as there were still not many cars about after petrol rationing. However about this time their number began to increase rapidly, and I soon came to the conclusion that no dog, no matter how well trained, should ever be off the lead in any place open to motor traffic and I have never seen any reason to change my mind.

Toffee naturally adored her walks, and always went berserk as soon as she knew we were going out. Well, all of my dogs have done that, but it took Toffee to think what she could do to hurry up the necessary preparations. Her answer was to bolt upstairs to the loo and hurl the door open ready for my invariable visit.!

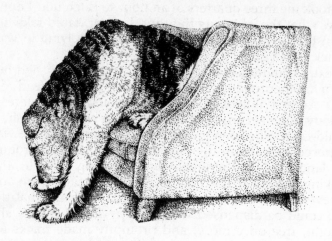

6
More Toffee

Even walking Toffee on the lead was no sinecure. Her passionate interest in everything kept her darting from left to right and back again, varied by dashes both forward and back, guaranteeing the lead twisting round my ankles and threatening to upset me. If a leaf fell she dived after it, if a bird flew over she was up on her hind legs trying to reach it, and she never missed even the quietest cat in the largest garden. While I was stronger than in Bamu's early days I was still no Amazon. Toffee was very large and tremendously strong, and I felt we were unequally matched.

I certainly couldn't cope with her on the lead once we had left the streets and she felt the grass beneath her feet, so she had to be let loose. Then she became what I believe the Americans call 'a running fool'. We had a proverb in our house which was simply 'Toffee always gets worse'. And she did. She would start those free runs not unlike a normal dog, dashing about examining points of interest, conducting lively running battles with Bamu, and so forth. But at the point where another dog would have begun to settle down and behave a little more sedately Toffee began to get into her stride. And disappear.

At first she would merely disappear, so to speak, in the vicinity, and at long intervals flash across our path, when we could catch her if we were quick – and lucky. Then she would stand with sides heaving and breath sawing in her throat; yet no matter how hot the day she was wild to be let go again. Sometimes having caught her like this we could keep the lead on until her breathing was normal again, in the hope that after the excitement had died out of her she would be content to stay with us in a civilized manner for the rest of the walk. It never worked. Her legs seemed to be possessed of an insatiable life of their own, and as soon as the lead was off they whipped the rest of her away like a conjuring trick.

The crux of the matter was that she wouldn't come when she was called. Only those who have suffered in this way – and I admit this is quite a large section of the dog-owning public – know the fury and frustration thus engendered in the conscientious owner to whom it is quite unthinkable to go home without his dog. Unfortunately one's natural and pardonable instinct when one does at last get one's talons on the miscreant is to flay the hide off it. This provides instant relief to the sufferer like a gulp of fresh air to a drowning man, but is not only followed by feelings of guilt and shame, but ensures that the torment will be infinitely more prolonged next time. In other words you are teaching the dog that it will pay him not to get caught.

I did once attempt to thrash Toffee when she escaped and led me a dance all over the district while in the middle of a heavy wash-day, but I really hadn't the strength to make much impression on her. I was once advised, and by a well-known trainer too, to 'thrash her until she couldn't stand'. With a dog as tough as Toffee it would have required real brutality to achieve such a result and that's just not my sort of thing. Also I doubt if it would have had the desired result. More probably it would have destroyed that unflappable affability which not only made her lovable, but bearable. A *vicious* Toffee could have had only one future – a short one.

In any case I feel this advice threw more light on the character of the giver than on my problem. For not long after this the trainer's collie began to evince a rooted distaste for his society, shooting out of the Obedience ring as soon as the lead was removed, and bolting for home when released for exercise in the park. As it was a highly trained prizewinning dog it appeared to me that his methods were rather expensively self-defeating.

I did at one stage buy a cane for use on Toffee in the house. It surprises me how many owners have one as a matter of course. Personally I considered it a token of defeat and would be ashamed to mention it but for one thing. Toffee did learn to dodge when she saw it in my hands, but if, as sometimes happened, I couldn't get to it fast enough and grabbed the poker instead, she simply stood and laughed at me. She thought it was highly comical (and it probably was) because she knew perfectly well that I wouldn't hit her with such a thing. The cane was never an effective deterrent, and in the end Toffee sensibly chewed it up, thereby relieving me of an embarrassment.

This reminds me that Toff was fond of chewing wood. She never attacked the furniture, fortunately, but newly planted trees were apt to be discovered neatly chewed off flat to the ground. It was impossible to leave a fire laid without her abstracting all the sticks of firewood for her own purposes, and when I tried to chop wood she would drive me mad by bouncing round me barking. As fast as the sticks flew up from the chopper she caught them and with her mighty jaws reduced them to matchwood.

When you opened Toff's mouth her great strong white teeth seemed to run back right down her throat. She had an extra incisor – seven in the upper jaw – and although we never got round to counting her molars there certainly seemed to be more than strictly necessary. We reckoned that she was part alligator, which not only accounted for her extra tooth (or teeth) but for the extra vertebrae which we felt sure were secreted along her spinal column.

An Airedale ideally has a short back. Toffee had a long one. Physically she was practically perfect from her hard inquisitive nose to the end of her long deep rib cage. From there backwards nothing was right. Her back went on and on, her tail curled where it should have been straight, her stifles were poker-straight when they should have been bent. As a result her action was not in the least like that of a terrier but something more like a prairie wolf. She had a magnificent head with gentle dark eyes and an expression like an archbishop at prayer, especially when she was up to no good.

Toffee could do the oddest things with her backbone, which was probably held together with elastic. She could lie on both sides at once and frequently did. By this I mean that she would lie on her back, then let her head and fore-legs flop blissfully on one side while her back end rested tranquilly on the other.

Like many great men of phenomenal energy she had the gift of utter repose while resting. She wasn't allowed on the chairs but worked it out that it didn't count as long as she kept her front feet on the floor. I have a photograph of her sitting on a low chair like this, fast asleep with her chin almost touching her forepaws, and the whole dog apparently hung up by the shoulders to dry.

Sometimes the need for complete relaxation would get the better of her. Then she would wriggle her bottom to the rear of the chair until it was comfortably supporting her spine, one long foreleg stretched luxuriously along the arm. She looked like some old club-man, the dignity of the pose somewhat marred by her two hind feet sticking up in front like a Disney rabbit, and the whole pose translated clean into Wonderland by her head being dropped right over the back of the chair, so that from any other angle she appeared to have been decapitated. Incomparable Toff.

Besides being mentally brilliant Toffee was an embarrassment in a class of her own, constantly reddening our cheeks with incidents which ranged from the trivial to the traumatic. There was the time when she swung round and glared at her own tail end with an accusing expression. We had some rather proper guests at the time who were evidently not at all puzzled by this behaviour, because a passing car had made an unfortunate and penetrating sound for which she was only too obviously taking the blame. From such minor faux pas as these to the major: such as the time when she allowed a Labrador to mate her on a very public footpath. The latter incident, by the way, took place on the twenty-eighth-day of her season and a full week after she had been proclaimed 'finished'.

I can't be the only one who will never forget the day when she was rashly included in a club team selected to challenge a fairly distant town in an Obedience match. Naomi had long ago given Toffee in disgust to her brother, and to his eternal credit he had taken over her training. So Stephen, myself and the two Airedales boarded the team coach with every expectation of an enjoyable day. Unfortunately Toff's own expectations went not to her head but to her bowels, and she commenced to have diarrhoea as only Toffee could. This lasted for the whole journey, which took three or four hours.

It was a pleasant seaside town and lovely weather, but we were appalled to find that the match was being held on a sports field. That's how green we were. Because we had always attended *indoor* training classes it hadn't occurred to us that a match could be held in the open.

We knew what would happen and Toffee didn't disappoint us. Her mind wasn't on the Heel on Lead, and when the lead was removed for Heel Free she promptly took off, pausing only to pass a motion, which gave Stephen a chance to catch her. The same thing happened in the Recall and again on the Retrieve. I believe she did the Sit and Flat Stays all right, and the judge spoke kindly to Stephen about her supposed indisposition, but as she had lost over half her marks she made a noble contribution to our team's defeat. But with no diminution of her happy spirits she much enjoyed her share of the refreshments provided, and even more enjoyed the walk we took along the beach before embarking for our journey home.

The one certain ingredient in the original composition of the Airedale was the Otterhound, and it is from this that the Airedale should derive its love of swimming. Many haven't, more's the pity, but no one could fault Toff on this score.

She plunged into the ocean with a fearlessness and *élan* which put the rest of the team to shame. We encouraged this, as we felt that it would sweeten her person and make for a quieter trip home, and when we eventually got her out of the water we put her on the lead to ensure her presence in the coach.

The sun soon dried her short coat. It was a very pleasant esplanade, red brick, trafficless, bounded by the cliff at the rear and the sea wall in front. Surely it was safe for Toff to enjoy a last short run? We weakened, off came the lead and she leapt straight through a gap in the sea wall and into the rising tide six feet below. There she swam gaily around until Stephen clambered down an iron ladder and somehow or other managed to lug her back up it and on to the red bricks once more.

We loaded her on to the coach still oozing sea. We felt that our troubles must now be over, but no! Incredibly, as soon as the vehicle got under way, she began to be ill again and the homeward journey was a repetition of the outward one.

I was once asked to tea by some charming friends who insisted that I bring both dogs. I warned them that Toffee was not a desirable guest but they would take no denial. They had a beautiful little Victorian cottage, lovingly renovated, and wanted to show it to me. They also owned two diminutive poodles and pointed out that as their garden was wired to contain these two tinies it was unlikely that Toffee could get out of it.

When we arrived they suggested that I look round the garden – 'Let the dogs go, they'll be quite all right' – before going indoors. Well, Toff and I saw simultaneously that the poodle-proof wire netting was only two feet high and was topped by nothing more impenetrable than a hedge. No hedge ever trimmed was a barrier to Toff, and her forefeet were already plunged in its foliage when I let out a despairing yell. At this she fortunately turned her head, and in doing so the ornamental lily pool caught her eye. Irresistible – the hedge could wait. She altered course in mid-air and leapt into the water.

By some mistake the pond had been dug four feet deep. Toffee submerged completely before coming to the surface gaudily bedizened with water-weed and goldfish. And to put it baldly, she ponged.

Our hosts, bless them, torn between laughter and dismay, rose to the occasion magnificently. 'Bring her into the kitchen and dry her,' they said, 'We've got *black* dog towels.' Well we did our best. Luckily she was in short summer trim, and if not exactly fragrant, was soon dry enough for our hosts to invite us to take her into their pretty sitting-room where they were setting out a sumptuous tea.

'Let her go,' they said, 'There's nothing she can hurt.' Rashly we did as we were bid, realising too late that a magnificent chocolate sponge had been placed on a low coffee table, which to Toffee was the same as the floor, since she could look down on it instead of having to reach up. Toff *did* have a nice time, and our hosts were absolutely charming. They did at least get a few laughs out of their party, but we weren't invited again and no wonder.

According to Konrad Lorenz in *Man Meets Dog*, the highest evidence of intelligence in a dog is the ability to tell a lie. Toffee provided an example which would have delighted the professor, one summer evening when I was sitting reading alone with the dogs. Bamu had unearthed an extremely dated marrow bone from the garden and was working away at it with gusto. Toffee was naturally coveting it with equal gusto, as expressed in a series of agonised groans, muted moos and tortured shiftings of her carcass on the carpet. I was well into my book and took no notice beyond the odd grunted 'Shut up Toff' and 'You wait till she's finished with it.'

But why should Toffee wait when she was capable of better things? She leapt to her feet and rushed to the French window bellowing 'CATS!' at the top of her voice. Bamu naturally dropped the bone and joined her. I reluctantly got up and opened the window so that they could clear our sacred garden of trespassing felines, but to my surprise only one dog hurtled through and across the lawn. Toffee, Toffee the inveterate cat chaser, stepped quietly aside to let her mother pass, then like a flash grabbed the bone, which she actually took to another room to enjoy lest it be restored to its rightful owner.

No bone on earth could have stopped Toffee if there had really been a cat there. The whole thing was simply a put-up job.

However if Toffee could tell a lie she could also tell the truth when needed. One morning she woke me early by a recitative of moos and bellows from Stephen's room. He happened to be away from home for a few days, but she and a half-grown pup that he had at the time still slept in their usual place. In the case of Chai the puppy this was an old armchair by Stephen's bed.

Repeated requests to 'Shut up Toff' producing no result, I got out of bed cursing and went to see what she wanted. To my surprise I found that the youngster had been dismembering her chair and in the process a spring had sprung – right out of the upholstery and into her cheek via her open mouth. She was in fact impaled, and had frozen motionless and soundless in that position, but Toffee, who had realised she was in a bad spot, had simply stood in the open doorway, and roared for help, not for herself but for her young rival. She was obviously pleased when I released the youngster – there was no meanness in Toffee at all.

Returning to the subject of bones, Toffee and Bamu never fell out over them although they are a very common cause of fighting among dogs. Nevertheless it was rather comical when I bought marrow bones for them, which I did every weekend. One bone would always be larger than the other, and I had to be careful to give the larger one to little Bamu and the smaller one to Toffee. They would carry them to the two opposing doormats – Bamu to the front and Toffee to the back – where they would put them down and give them an exploratory lick. Next, with heads down, they would glare at each other, then as if at a signal each would leave her own bone and in one mad rush through hall and kitchen would leap on the other's bone and claim it. Thus each got the bone appropriate to her size and was at the same time satisfied that she had asserted herself and pulled a fast one on her partner.

All this time the battle of the Recall was going on. I don't think there was any method of teaching this that we didn't try on Toffee except the long range electric collar whereby one can give the dog slight electric shocks by means of a control held in the hand. I had read about these but had no idea where to get one. It might have worked – and if it had it would have been a mighty big feather in the cap of its inventor, because nothing else did.

All the common or garden methods were a failure for the simple reason that Toff didn't notice we were using them, her attention being elsewhere. I refer to such ploys as calling, whistling, scolding, praising, cajoling, running away or hiding behind trees. If she thought of them at all I suppose she assumed we were merely amusing ourselves, but not that it had any direct application to her good self.

She developed what we called her 'backyard complex'. This meant that to Toffee any place within ten miles of home was her backyard, therefore she couldn't get lost in it and was at liberty to get back indoors at any time she pleased – the early hours of the morning, for instance. Under the circumstances she was hardly likely to care whether we were hiding behind trees or standing on our heads on the top of the Eiffel Tower. Our only comfort was that she never got into trouble on her rambles. She never fought or bit, and as her mania was for open country she never ran about the roads. Luckily there were no sheep near us, though I daresay she treed a few cats in the woods.

Once we actually kept her on the lead for an entire year on the principle that the whole thing might just be a bad habit and that we might be able to break it and start afresh. It didn't work, of course. By the end of the first week she was right back to her old form.

We also tried the reverse, taking her for two weeks down to a lovely Welsh farm where the fields ran right down to the beach, and where she could enjoy almost unlimited freedom. Trying to use a little intelligent antici-pation I decided that we – myself, the two children and the two dogs – had better travel on the night train. This meant that Toffee spent the entire preceding day in a frenzy of excitement, tearing up and down the stairs and constantly upsetting our packing by disembowelling all the cases.

When evening came we first had to take a train up to town. This was difficult enough, but much worse was the journey across London by tube. Toffee had never been on the Underground before and relished every second of it – the stairs, the lifts, the lights, the wonderful noises and that strange intriguing smell. This part of our progress was made especially hazardous by Toffee's picking up a drunk. She had a specially strong magnetism for the intoxicated: possibly her beaming countenance and honest egotism restored their faith in life. Anyway we had great difficulty in getting rid of this one, who assured us with many tears that he had had an old dog just like her, which I very much doubted. If he had, though, it could have explained what had driven him to drink. Toff of course played up to him with a sickening sentimentality; she was never the dog to waste a good fan.

Somehow we prised these two dear old pals apart and found our train already waiting. It was midnight, departure was timed for one o'clock, and it was already packed tight! With sinking hearts we climbed aboard and began to force our way down the corridor against a barrage of murderous glares from the passengers already installed.

Eventually I sighted a carriage where there was actually a vacant seat, so I steered my charges in. I made Naomi sit down as she had recently been in hospital with a bad back, and Steve and I prepared to straphang through the night.

But lo and behold a miracle! The Miracle of the Mad Guard, no less, who appeared, foaming with rage, and accused the *other* passengers of tearing the Ladies Only sticker off the window. He would listen to no denials but ejected the lot – who were mostly women anyway. He took not an atom of notice of *our* assorted party, containing as it did two large dogs and one teenage boy, but muttered fiercely in his whiskers and *locked us in*. Why? Who knows? I don't for one minute believe that the other unfortunates had even seen any Ladies Only stickers, much less tampered with them. As for the two children, there were plenty of other children on the train, all travelling in extreme discomfort, I should say.

I can only conclude that he was of that strange breed of dyed-in-the-wool if not always very reasonable animal lovers. I assume that he felt it his mission to protect our two frail pets trapped in the Gehenna of his grossly overcrowded train. If that was his end he certainly achieved it. Angry passengers pounded on the inner door, but we were powerless to renounce the spacious luxury of our 'private compartment' – he didn't open the door until we were well into Wales. Just as well we didn't want to alight in England, for our sainted Mad Guard never addressed a single word to us and we never saw him again.

I spoke of luxury. Well – Naomi spent the night flat on her poor back, using the entire length of one seat. Steve and I occupied the other. But whereas Naomi had at least the chance of a little sleep, we two were entered upon a gruelling test of endurance, for Toffee, with a vim and vigour unimpaired by her non-stop activity of the preceding eighteen hours, spent the entire night trying to climb out of the window. She was only prevented by Stephen and myself, a vigil which effectually put an end to any foolish ideas we might have had about taking the odd nap ourselves.

When we arrived bleary-eyed in Swansea, released without a word by the Mad Guard, we found the buses were on strike – and we still had eighteen miles to go. We staggered along to the market place, where we were lucky to find a farmer who lived close to our destination and who was willing to carry us the rest of the way in the back of his Land Rover. Toffee loved this as it smelt strongly of sheep. This enlivened her still further and she spent most of the trip hanging half-way over the tailboard.

Poor Toff. The glorious fields, dunes and beaches of the Gower were paradise to her. She was possibly happier during that fortnight than any dog has ever been since dogs were created. One day we wandered from one end of Rhossili Bay to the other and back again, wading in the edge of the sea the whole length of the beach, three miles long by a mile wide and in many places carpeted with sea-gulls. We took a long time over it, talking, laughing, and examining the shells and seaweeds as we walked. During all those hours Toffee was galloping flat out, ranging from end to end of the beach and across and across it.

Apart from the gulls we had it to ourselves. They rose in screaming clouds as she scattered them, and contempt-uously flew over the water towards the open sea. The sea was very shallow for a long way out and it was surprising how far Toffee could cleave the waves at a gallop before getting out of her depth. When she did, she would turn and come back. She was no fool and knew she stood more chance on foot than swimming: she did actually catch a seagull once in a rock pool. It couldn't have seen her coming.

All in all, Toff behaved pretty well on that holiday. In fact it was my sainted Bamu who blotted her copy-book by killing an in-lay hen which suddenly sprang out of the grass at her feet. Our long-suffering landlady told us that it was one from a batch hidden by the mother hen in the field. No one knew she had them until she proudly led them into the farmhouse one day. But now and again one of the chicks, long after they were grown up, would wan-der off to their birthplace, no doubt for old times' sake. Unhappily Bamu's victim had been indulging in just such a nostalgic potter when I was on the point of putting Bamu on the lead before getting too near the farmyard.

All too soon our two weeks were up and we set sail for home. This time we got the bus to Swansea without any trouble and filled in the time before the train went by hav-ing a look round the market again. There was a man there selling a litter of Welsh collie puppies. Eight weeks old he said, but I think they were nearer four. He was asking twenty-five shillings for the dogs and fourteen for the bitches. I thought it would round off the holiday nicely if we took one home, kept it for a week or two to condition it and then sold it to a good home as a contribution to my impending vet's bill.

Some contribution was necessary because I remember counting the contents of my purse four times before I was absolutely certain that this interesting business venture was financially possible. I picked a very fetching light blue merle bitch pup and the man gave me a cardboard box to carry her in. I bought a very large local paper to use as bedding, then we went into a market café, where we bought a glass of cold milk which we decanted into Naomi's leak-proof beaker, and so went off to catch the train. I believe we had about one and tenpence left between us, but my husband was to meet us at the London terminus and would have the privilege of paying our fares from there.

We had a pleasant journey home. Toffee was quite sub-dued for once – I think she had decided to live for ever on the Gower and was a little put out by her involuntary change of plan. We all got seats quite easily. Bamu was as angelic as ever, and Rosie, as we named our infant com-panion, attracted a good deal of pleasant comment from our fellow travellers.

It was rather hot in the carriage, and Rosie panted a little, so I offered her some of the milk in Toffee's bowl. She lapped it enthusiastically, and after some rather floppy attempts to play with Stephen's fingers, fell asleep. This sequence was repeated at intervals all through the long journey home. She was able to relax comfortably in her lidless cardboard box. The newspaper became rather damp, but did not leak or become smelly, and altogether we felt it had been a very successful venture so far.

Of course, buying a puppy in a market place – any mar-ket place – is one of the very worst ways to acquire one, but it is also a very romantic one. I'd always had a sneak-ing desire to do it, and just that once I did. On the whole it turned out more successfully than I had any right to expect, due mainly to Rosie's excellent heritage from tough working parents.

Our first snag came when our avid milk-lapper of the train made it obvious that she had never been weaned and had only drunk because it had been so hot. We couldn't get her to take anything at all. She was also, like most collie puppies, too inquisitive and too busy to have time for such a dull pursuit.

I got over this by continually proffering tiny titbits for the first day – mostly licked off my fingers, which were much more to her taste than any dish. On the principle that anything is better than nothing she got an extraordinary assortment in minute quantities that day. Butter, cream, gravy, fishpaste – I didn't much care what it was so long as she took it voluntarily. I was teaching her to eat, even though she only got through about a tablespoonful of very mixed food that first day. By the end of the first week she had learnt so well that she would both eat and drink from a bowl on the floor.

Under her pretty fluff she was very thin and she scratched a good deal. I diagnosed worms but thought another week or two's careful rearing would make worming a safer operation. But I did look into her coat and was horrified to see that she was literally covered all over with lice. We thought they must have been poultry lice as they were pure white, packed shoulder to shoulder, and some were very much smaller than others. I've certainly never seen anything quite like them before or since, whatever they were. Hoping to save Rosie from a bath Naomi worked for two hours with a pair of tweezers, removing these unwanted passengers by hand. At last she had to give up in despair. 'This poor puppy's got more lice than she's got hairs – and I mean that literally,' she said.

So I took a chance and bathed her in a pretty strong insecticidal wash which I had often used with great success on my adults. Of course I rinsed her very well indeed, but she still smelt quite distinctly of her unorthodox shampoo even after she had been thoroughly combed and dried. Not that it worried Rosie – I suspect she was having a whale of a time. Completely rid of her all-embracing lice and a little later of two or three hundred worms, her appetite improved and her energy and high spirits were quite inexhaustible. Moreover she looked good enough to eat, with her exquisitely coloured fluff and bright eyes (still blue) like some precious toy from a Christmas tree.

I now felt Rosie was ready to go to a good home, and

she soon found enthusiastic new owners. They were quite enchanted with with their new baby, so it came as something of a shock to me to receive an anxious call from them a week or two later to tell me that all her coat had fallen out! I owned up about the shampoo and described the reason for using it in some detail. This was relayed to Rosie's new vet, who, although he said it was undoubtedly the cause of her hair falling out, was kind enough to add that the lice would have been difficult to eradicate and that my over-stern measures had certainly achieved that!

Fortunately her new owners were still thrilled with her and a year later sent me a photograph of a lissom and shining Rosie with good health and happiness gleaming from every hair of a long and luxuriant coat.

This little episode of Rosie made an interesting postscript to our holiday, but as far as poor Toffee was concerned her two weeks of bliss was almost tragic in its consequence. Remember that we had hoped that virtually unlimited freedom and her fill of running might get the tickle out of her feet and sate her appetite for the wide open spaces? No, it didn't work. Every day she had run faster and farther, her body had acquired a steely strength and tautness, and by the end of the fortnight she was nearly wild.

Bamu was a little subdued, as we all were, with that slightly let-down feeling one gets at the end of an extra-enjoyable holiday. But poor Toffee was almost suicidal. Throwing herself into her grief with her usual single-mindedness she spent most of her time upstairs, where I could hear her grieving, groaning and sobbing. Her agony of mind was very real, even allowing for her habit of overacting any part she chose to play. She took no notice of Rosie at all, she only wanted to be out and free. When she *was* out and free she was worse than ever: probably she had formed an escape plan which involved running all the way back to the Gower. It had been a wonderful holiday for all of us and an experience we would not have missed, but as a cure for Toffee's misdemeanours it came very low down on the scoreboard of success.

As it was her marathon runs had affected her heart – the

vet diagnosed Athlete's Heart, an enlargement caused by over-exercise. I was faced with the choice of keeping her always on the lead for her own good, or letting her go on the principle of a short life and a merry one. I decided on the latter as it would certainly have been Toff's own choice. Not that she was finished, not by a long shot. As witness the morning when I came downstairs to find that she had chewed up my false teeth which had rashly been left within reach.

Shamefacedly presenting them to the dentist I wasn't surprised when he asked 'My goodness, whatever happened to these?'

'The dog got them,' I muttered.

'Oh well,' he said cheerfully, 'Puppies will be puppies.'

Which stung me to reply 'But this puppy is nine years old.'

Toffee always gets worse, we said. It's true that in her old age she became so addicted to free ranging in the woods that whenever we took her out she rarely came home before six the next morning. Once she failed to reappear at all, and eventually I rang the police station. They had her, because she had attached herself to an elderly couple who had turned her in and were highly indignant that such a lovely dog should have owners heartless enough to let her wander on her own. We always removed her collar when unleashing her for fear she would become entangled in some distant thicket and die a worse death than she deserved.

We were so amazed to hear that the station sergeant was actually afraid of her because she snarled at him so savagely, that it struck us as a joke, and an incredible one at that; but on looking back I can quite see that being thrown into clink must have come as a terrible shock to this child of the wide open spaces.

Toffee also got worse in the matter of escaping. It became an obsession which nearly drove me out of my mind. I literally could not take my eyes off her, and it became a great strain.

First of all I constructed in the garden a running line complete with dangling lead so that I could safely leave her to spend a penny while I did the washing up or whatever. Result – nil. She stood as if frozen in the very attitude she was in when hooked on. And proceeded to give a recitative of heartrending moos.

Relenting, I felt I must sacrifice the washing up or whatever and remain on sentry duty till the penny was spent. Result – no pennies. That fiendish dog would control herself for twenty-four hours or more rather than relieve herself while I was watching – not that she was shy, much less modest, but because the penny was a mere pawn in the game. The game being 'I'm watching you' versus 'The minute you take your eyes off me I'm gone.'

Not being naturally patient I was weak enough on several occasions to use these dreary minutes to get a scuttle of coal from the bunker, thinking that I would be able to watch her just as well – or at least that she would think I was.

But it never did to underestimate Toffee. She was well aware that she who mines coal from a bunker must most of the time use both her eyes for the job, and no matter how short the interval I would invariably look up again to see with a shock of surprise Toffee cavorting in the next garden and then it was goodbye, Toff, until tomorrow morning.

She was really a full time job, and I just didn't have the time. My marriage had broken up, both children had left school and were away from home, Stephen working as an apprentice Guide Dog Trainer and Naomi at Cambridge doing a teacher's training course. Stephen had been especially useful with the dogs, especially Toffee, with whom he had a very deep love-hate relationship. He had given her lots of runs, often slipping out of his bedroom window with her (it was on the ground floor) and taking to the woods for a few hours.

Oddly enough she would stay with him on these nocturnal rambles. I used to think she did this because she wanted his protection, but when I remember the nights out she spent alone I realise I wronged her and that she must really have been keeping an eye on him for his own sake.

Stephen got a great kick out of these walks, not least because he believed I was ignorant of them and would have forbidden them. Actually I knew all about them from the start and didn't mind at all. I felt they were giving him an outlet made necessary by the upheaval in our domestic life. Besides, he was now a big lad and I had no doubt of his ability to look after himself. As for Toffee, it had long ago become obvious that she bore a charmed life.

It is understandable therefore that she was increasingly restless, but that wasn't all. In her old age her lifetime obsession became almost a disease. She thought of nothing else, never missed the ghost of a chance and needed watching all the time.

In an endeavour to be sensible and practical for once in my life I had got a job in a shop, but was fired at the end of three weeks. I was given to understand quite clearly that this was not so much because I often made mistakes when giving change as because these mistakes were usually in the customer's favour.

It was then I decided that it would be safer (and much more fun) to try making a living out of that hobby which was already second nature to me. I still had some trimming customers. I had always had a few. So I bought a good pair of clippers with my fast-diminishing resources. As I could not stay indefinitely in my house I began looking round for suitable premises to start boarding kennels. I found them and they included half an acre of very rough old orchard, unfenced.

Naturally this would have to be remedied, but a mere fence was not going to contain Toffee. If you can't keep a dog in a tight little suburban garden you are not going to keep it in a whole orchard, where the fence is many times longer and any dog with a taste for the greener grass is usually going to be invisible anyway.

Also there were one or two trigger-happy farmers about with a sharp eye on their sheep. No good refusing to face facts. Toffee would have been shot for sheep chasing before we had been there a week. Her heart was also deteriorating and I still had my nightmare about her dying out in the country somewhere and my never knowing what had become of her.

I really was at the end of my tether. Toffee was in her tenth year when I took her to the vet's, where she died, happy to the last, in my arms.

Of course I regretted it the moment it was done, even though I knew I really had no choice. For more than nine years Toffee had been one of the most important factors in my life, if only because she represented the perpetual need to outwit her. And though I never doubted the power of her intellect, I don't believe even I quite realised it until she was gone. She was a person, and while I always feel that I have lost a child when a dog dies, this time I felt instead that I had lost an adult. Without realizing it I had been subconsciously aware that there was always another independent mind in the house, thinking its own thoughts and pursuing its own interests instead of mostly reflecting myself and my moods.

In spite of all the hard work and worry she had given me Toffee was a most lovable dog. In spite of all her pre-occupations she always had time for affection. She was also a dog who compelled admiration from all who saw her. With her noble head and fearless demeanour, how could we not be proud of her?

We once saw a film in which one cowboy said to another who was having trouble controlling his mettle-some mount, 'That's a lot of horse you've got there.' Well, Toffee was a lot of dog. I could write a book about her alone and she will crop up again in later chapters of this one.

I shall never see her like again.

7

Chai and Peggy

It was about this time that I lost my dear little Bamu. Apart from killing that one hen I never knew her to step out of line. She came to me as a sickly and undersized puppy who could so easily have died in uncaring hands, at a time when I myself was not in much better case physically. Consequently she adored me as her salvation, while the glowing feeling that she kindled in me warmed me as nothing else had for years, and set me on the road to recovery.

She was also the ancestress of all my present dogs, and to all the puppies of her line she gave something of her own ideal nature and beautiful coat.

But her bad start in life had always told on her strength and she began to be very old indeed long before time. I'm not quite certain now whether she went before Toffee or not, but I believe she must have died a little before her daughter.

I just didn't know what I was going to do without her,

and would have done anything in my power to have kept her going for even another month. I couldn't spare her, it was as simple as that. But in spite of visits to the vet, in spite of all I could do, she was failing rapidly. My vet told me she had creeping paralysis – some mornings she would wake with her paws curled under and it was sometimes very hard to get them down to meet the floor properly so that she could walk. Tablets helped her with this and then I found she was passing no motions because she had no feeling in her hind part to tell her what was needed. So I had to tell her myself, going out into the garden with her to tell her 'Be Quick'. This made her spend a penny and she would have then returned to the house but for my repeated urgings of the command. It was only because she knew what I meant and as ever wanted to please me that she would then squat, and with the aid of generous dosings of liquid paraffin all would be well.

But repeated heart attacks soon increased her weakness, and before long she could only breathe when propped up with cushions. There was only one thing to do and I did it. She was eleven and had been blind for several years, although this affliction came on her too slowly to be much of a trial to her, she adjusted so well. It was strange that in the woods she never ran into trees or low spreading branches. If she was using radar she switched it off when she got home, for there she would crash into anything left out of place, for instance a wheelbarrow left carelessly in the dogs' flight path from the back door.

The double loss of Toffee and Bamu, although it left me feeling very low, did not leave me dogless. Stephen had been promised a puppy from Toffee's last litter, but unfortunately the only bitch (provisionally named Superpup) did not live. He was naturally very disappointed, so with the proceeds from this litter I bought him a well-bred puppy from a top kennel which we hoped would make a foundation bitch for showing and breeding. After a lot of thought he named her Chai, which is a Romany word roughly equivalent to Lassie.

Moreover I had acquired a young West Highland White bitch as I thought it would be wise to have a small breed as a second string. I had a feeling that Westies were destined to be popular, and at least had the satisfaction of being dead right, for they zoomed up the popularity ratings and have been somewhere near the top ever since.

This little Highlander was incredibly named Fifi, which I promptly changed to Peggy, which suited her much better. She must have approved the change because she answered to it immediately.

She was eighteen months old, very subdued and not at all fond of walks. Her pads were quite pink and beautifully clean. Never having had a white dog before I thought nothing of this until I noticed them darkening and her eagerness to go out increasing. Then the reason for the pinkness became apparent – she had never been exercised before. I discovered later that her previous owners' other dogs would not have her in the house so she had been kept in a rabbit hutch at the end of a long garden.

Toffee and Bamu, as always, had welcomed her kindly, while Chai, now nearly full-grown, was quite crazy about her and soon made it clear that this little white dog was *her* little white dog.

We were relieved to see this as Chai was already showing signs of being rather an odd dog. When still a fluffy bundle of puppy she had worried me rather by 'squirrelling', i.e. making hoards of doggy treasures and hiding them away so that no one else could have them. I'd come across them in odd corners, behind the settee or even under the carpet. She made no objection when I turfed them out and distributed them to the others, but in a day or two I would come across the same collection again.

Another more worrying trait appeared when she was about six months old. A friend came in to show us her new poodle puppy. I called Chai to come and see it, for it is natural for puppies to love each other, the younger the better. Luckily for this snowy scrap it was still uninoculated and its Mum was therefore carrying it chest high, for Chai spotted it the instant she came into the garden, and immediately flew at it, leaving no possible doubt as to her intentions.

Of course, I pulled her off and held her, and apart from

81

my embarrassment no harm was done.

A more amusing foible was her attitude to Naomi's collection of small toys and models which she kept on a shelf of her bedroom bookcase. One was a delicious little donkey made of grey felt with a scarlet saddle and embroidered harness. It was a daily routine with Chai to sneak up to her room and move him. Sometimes she only moved him a few inches further along the shelf, sometimes Naomi would find him in the middle of her bed. He was never chewed or otherwise harmed, but it was obvious that he must soon lose his pristine freshness if this continued.

We came to the conclusion that Chai had become a member of some obscure religious order and believed she must perform this ritual action every day or something terrible would befall her.

One day Naomi came home with a new model – a little carved wooden warthog. She was giving it an exhaustive polishing when Chai came up to see what she was doing. It happened that the tail end was towards Chai and she sniffed it curiously.

'Want to see him, Chai?' asked Naomi and turned him head-towards. Then a very strange thing happened. As soon as Chai caught sight of that terrible frowning visage with its wrinkled snout and curling tusks she put her tail down and flew for her life! It made no difference that the head was less than two inches long, coloured chestnut red and smelt pleasantly of furniture polish. Intrigued, Naomi called her back and soon discovered that she could make her approach or back off smartly by presenting either end of her new toy.

She was studying biology and was tremendously impressed by the effectiveness of what she called 'the aggression pattern' even on the face of a model so small. And then she stood Warthog on the shelf beside the little donkey 'to protect him'. And protect him he did. Chai never moved the little donkey again!

Another important tenet of Chai's religion was a strong taboo on electric fires. She was obviously forbidden to go anywhere near them, whether alight or not. This dogma proved useful to me on several occasions. The chief of these was when Peggy produced her first and only litter in the spare bedroom. Peggy was a much more devoted mother in the first two weeks than any of my other bitches had been. I had to pick her up off her puppies and carry her downstairs and into the garden to relieve herself.

This was all right as it meant the door could be kept shut at all times, essential as we now knew that Chai was a potential puppy killer. She just hated all the little brats on principle. The difficulty arose when Peg felt she could leave her little pink-and-white sons long enough to attend to her other duties. If the door was shut I often failed to hear her scratching and whining to be let out, and in any case it meant two trips upstairs, first to let her out and then to shut her in.

This was very inconvenient until genius struck – the answer was an electric fire. I stationed one, flex neatly coiled up, in the open doorway, and the problem was solved. Peggy didn't care a fig for Chai's taboos, and zipped gaily in and out as she pleased. As for Chai, not even the urge to commit infanticide could get her past this powerful juju. Peg's puppies were safe, thanks to this happy partnership between modern technology and ancient voodoo.

On another occasion Chai was with me when visiting a customer and she was invited in – after I had made sure that the family cat was not at home. Once in I discovered to my horror that this magnificent tortoiseshell-and-white puss was only just not at home – she was sitting on the doorstep outside a perfectly clear glass door and had not the slightest intention of moving. Grabbing Chai in a hurry I explained the situation – that door and puss would both last approximately five seconds after I let her go. I offered to put her back in the car, but it was hot and my customer wouldn't hear of it.

Just then I noticed an electric fire standing in a corner. Saved! To my customer's complete astonishment I placed it on the doormat and the problem ceased to exist. Chai could do no more than look longingly at her prospective prey, for she wouldn't go within four feet of the door now.

When faced with fencing my half acre of orchard Naomi

remarked that it was a pity we couldn't get hold of enough electric fires to go all round it as they would have confined Chai better than any fence ever built.

It was when she turned six months that I really began to worry about Chai. She didn't seem to be growing at all and was terribly moody and miserable at times. Then I noticed that during these spells her neck glands were swollen, so off we went to the vet.

At first she could find nothing wrong, but when I mentioned the glands she felt them and was puzzled when further examination revealed that they were the *only* glands to be enlarged. Apparently it is usual for all the glands to be swollen if any are. She took two swabs for laboratory examination and sent them away although both looked perfectly clean.

It was nearly three weeks before the report came back. Chai did have some sort of very rare bug infecting her neck glands only. By the time all this was done and she had been treated and cured she was ten months old and very poor and weedy-looking. Her beautiful sturdy little legs had become starved and thin with pencil-like bones. Physically she picked up well. She filled out, put on height, and as sometimes happens, her bones thickened up in her late adolescence. Mentally, however, her nature seemed to have been warped. She was a miserable dog who seemed to enjoy nothing but a free run.

After we had moved I tried to get her and Peggy in whelp, but Peggy never had any more puppies, and Chai was a reluctant starter to say the least.

With a lot of help from my new vets she did eventually produce seven beautiful babies, and then my troubles really started. It had never occurred to me that her reaction to her own pups might be the same as to others, but it was. Her maternal instinct was too strong to allow her to leave them, yet she seemed to have a horror of them.

I have seen her go back to the box where they were asleep in the usual black-tipped-with-gold heap, and very carefully – furtively would be a better word – tiptoe into the opposite corner and sit in as small a space as she possibly could. 'Chai sitting on a sixpence' we used to call it.

But no matter how quiet and careful she was, she was never a match for her offspring's survival mechanism. Within seconds they would stir, and then the whole squeaking heap would flatten out and being creeping surprisingly fast across the box towards her. Then it was just a case of my being quicker than she was.

There was no question of leaving her to care for them in the normal way. They wouldn't have survived the first day. If I as much as wanted to put a kettle on I either had to get someone capable to watch her, or put her lead on and drag her into the kitchen until the job was done.

She had plenty of milk but not the least intention of letting them feed. I overcame this by making her lie on my bed and holding her down with one hand while picking the puppies out of the adjacent box and putting them to her one by one, undeterred by the fearsome snarling which accompanied the whole operation.

Night-time was a problem which I solved by keeping the box beside my bed and making her sleep on the eiderdown. Risking no accidents I kept her lead on and slept with the loop round my wrist under the bedclothes. Any time she got restless in the night she woke me and I was able to cope with whatever was needed. The main thing was that she got no chance for mass murder at midnight.

If I tried shutting her out of the bedroom she screamed the place down. I wonder she didn't have a nervous breakdown. Me too, but I believe very strongly that the breeder who causes puppies to be born is under a compelling moral obligation to keep them alive and do everything possible to ensure them a happy and successful future.

When they were four weeks old I put them out in the puppy kennel and I think Chai liked them better than at any other time. If she wanted to be near them she could sit by the wire, where they gathered enthusiastically on the other side, but were unable to pester her.

It suited Chai, but it didn't suit anybody else. My puppy kennel was fine for seven puppies to sleep in but hopelessly inadequate even with its small covered run for their daytime energies. It was in a beautiful tree-lined grass run which should have given them plenty of scope, but it was

January, with the nastiest sort of January weather.

We didn't have a lot of snow, but the wind was bitter, with sleet and hail and very often icy slush on the ground. I hated putting them out there for I felt they must be miserable and insufficiently protected from the elements.

In spite of this they thrived and became very strong and jolly puppies, although my vet told me they were a credit to me and not the bitch! I'm glad to remember now that I had taken the precaution of choosing an unshown (but extremely handsome) grandson of Bamu's for their father in order to improve on Chai's temperament. This was fortunately effective and none of them as far as I knew grew up like Chai, which confirmed my suspicion that her troubles dated, at least partly, from her gland infection.

Nevertheless I knew I couldn't go through all that again so I struck Chai off the active list. Peggy had already struck herself off, so there I was with two retired bitches drawing their pensions while they were still young and should have had some productive years still in front of them. And I was trying to start a business! We couldn't even show Chai, for, although she had grown into a beautiful dog in spite of a poor coat, on entering any show she would begin a barrage of blood-curdling growls which lasted until we went home and was audible everywhere, upsetting other exhibitors and embarrassing me horribly.

All this made me very lonely for Toffee and Bamu, for if you are a one-breed devotee nothing gives you a greater feeling of desolation than the sense that your own beloved breed has let you down.

What good is a gold-plated pedigree if you can't enjoy the resultant dog? Impeccable show points were for me at least a very poor consolation. I decided to let beauty go hang, and was fortunate enough to be able to get a granddaughter – possibly the very last – of Bamu's.

8
Solo

Candy Tuff was a bitch which I had sold as a puppy to a woman who later decided to breed, and in fact went on to found a whole kennel on this daughter of Bamu. She became also one of my first friends-through-breeding, and we had kept in close touch throughout Candy's career.

There had been two or three litters, containing some very fine Airedales with lovely temperaments, and when Chai proved such a disappointment to me and I was longing for my old Bamu, there was only one place to look for a puppy from her bloodline. But Candy was nearing the end of her productive life, and although mated she became very ill and the vet announced that her litter (if any) must have been lost.

Never give up hope! A week or so later Candy's owner rang me in great excitement to say that in spite of this edict she believed Candy was in whelp after all. Punctual to the day she produced three puppies, two girls and a boy. The vet frankly owned himself astonished and said they probably represented the puppies from one ovary only – the rest must have died as he said – and that it was nothing short of a miracle.

On being told this I asked for my little girl to be registered as Miss Miracle, and as Eladeria Miss Miracle she came to me, to have the 'of Caterways' added to her name later. That part was easy, it was much harder finding a name for everyday. Eventually I remembered that I had originally meant to buy two bitches from this litter but as I was only able to have this one I called her Solo.

She was only seven weeks old when she came to me, a very plain puppy with a skimpy coat and odd ears. None of that curly fluffy glamour which had made Chai so irresistible at that age. And when I say odd ears I mean that they simply weren't a pair. We know that the two most important original ingredients of the Airedale were the Otterhound and some sort of local terrier. Solo proved this true because she had an ear from each source – one beautiful perky terrier ear and one heavy hound ear!

Although this was a little disappointing because I would have liked to show her, before I had had her five minutes I couldn't have cared less if she had looked like a camel!

The first thing was to tell Chai in no uncertain terms that this was one puppy which must never be harmed, and if she so much as laid a tooth on her I would personally strangle her with my bare hands. She got the message and ignored the newcomer, in which she was aided by Solo herself. Solo was no fool, and she knew danger when she saw it. She kept clear, and if they ever did bump into each other she immediately gave Chai best, abased herself before her and gave her no excuse to let fly. Peggy used to play with her and hunt with Chai, but Solo's main interest in life was – me.

I had a lot of constructive work to do in setting up my boarding kennels. Solo followed me everywhere, intensely interested in everything, picking up my tools and introducing her little whiskerless nose just where the hammer was about to fall or the saw cut. I called it her 'six inches trouble' – she just had to have her snout within that distance of whatever I was doing.

Her little figure epitomized that spirit of courage and enquiry which always slays me about any Airedale puppy of sound breeding. They alway remind me of tiny boys about to explore the world, brave in their first tight suits of shorts and braces.

Plain Airedale puppies with skimpy coats nearly always put on suits of armour as they grow up, brilliant, hard and weatherproof. Glamorous curly balls of fluff too often become the owners of poor coats of weak dull hair, wishy-washy in colour, dusty grey and light fawn.

Solo had inherited Bamu's colour. Gleaming blueblack jacket and blazing red gold hair on legs and head – furnishings as they are called. I did take her to one big breed show, not because I thought she had a chance, but because I wanted to go and liked her company every bit as much as she liked mine.

I am sure the judge knew she was an also-ran as soon as she saw that head with its tell-tale ears and inch-long whiskers. She probably saw too the intelligence and gentleness in her bright dark eyes. At all events she handled her so gently and said to me 'Your girl has the finest colour of any dog here today.' Which made my show a success and for which I will always remember her gratefully.

I used to think those odd ears gave the clue to Solo's charm for me. Her nature combined in perfect balance the two distinct strains in the Airedale character. The lively ear showed a bold and fearless nature. Like Toff, she had no nerves but an insatiable curiosity and appetite for new places and experiences. But on the side of the ear that was carried modestly low she was intensely sensitive and loving, and like Bamu (certainly not like Toff) she was most deeply willing to be with me, help me and please me.

This combination made her gay, loving, self-confident and very obedient. We never argued and she was a joy to have with me, no matter where. And as our bond deepened with her increasing maturity, a strange thing happened. From mere pleasure in her society I began to take actual courage from having her beside me. It was like my childhood all over again, when the presence of Scamp helped me to overcome shyness and self-doubt and fool the world into believing that I believed in myself – and perhaps I did. This help came to me again from Solo, and I needed it because I was going through another very grim time in my life. But to step out with Solo made me straighten my back, lift my head and go on with fresh courage for my daily battle with life.

From the start Solo was every bit as happy as Toffee, perhaps even more so, for whereas Toffee could enjoy putting her all into moaning about her griefs, Solo never seemed to have any. You could see from just looking at her that she was always actively and consciously enjoying whatever was her lot at the time. You could leave her kicking about on her own in the orchard all day and she took it as a precious day's holiday with plenty to do. Or you could take her on the lead through a crowded market-place and she never missed a smell, sight or sound. She loved the car and was never sick in it. She loved going to the sea, she loved a rainy day and a well-earned snooze by the fire. I called her my 'go anywhere, do anything' dog.

She was also very intelligent. Not quite in Toffee's league, but as I have said, Toffee's genius really only benefited its owner. Solo's was there for my use whenever I needed it.

One day, without any provocation, Chai turned on Peggy and laid her head open for several inches. Peggy was in many ways an irritating little dog, although not responsible for this attack. She was very possessive. She always wanted to be fondled, and while I was quite willing for her to sit on my lap, I found it very annoying to have her continually clawing at my arm and demanding more and more fussing.

Worse than that, she was a stirrer. She made trouble between the other two and I lived in constant fear of an explosion which could have been very serious. On the whole I thought Peg would be better off in an individual home where she could have all the perks to herself.

I advertised locally, and asked the girl who applied to come and see her. She fell for her and I took her to them the next day as I wished to see where she was going. It was an ideal home with a young couple who had just moved into a small village where they had a house with a large walled garden. They wanted a dog they could cuddle and take for walks. All things considered, I think Peggy fell on her feet, and she must have thought so too, because the report I had was that she had not so much as looked after me as I walked out of the door. Not flattering to me, but then I suppose that a dog that has spent its first eighteen months alone in a rabbit hutch can hardly be expected to feel attachments in the same way as one which has lived in your house from babyhood and been treated from the first as one of the family.

I had to warn her new owners about one thing, which was Peggy's peculiar habit of spending her pennies in the house when she was in season. She was always perfectly clean at all other times, but when on heat she needed strict supervision and even got so wily that on the command 'Be quick' she would actually stoop down and *pretend* to be doing her duty. Then she would run straight back into the house in a beeline for the nearest rug! This put me to the indignity of having to bend down and watch carefully for actual results, while Peg showed the whites of her eyes as she kept a beady eye on me. At night of course I had to resort to a torch, held unwaveringly on 'X marks the spot'!

I knew that telling her prospective owners about this peccadillo might cut short their interest sharply, but then if they had been that sort what would have happened to Peg on the first occasion that she sinned? It would have been most unfair to the people too. No, I had to tell them and they were most grateful. They said it didn't matter as Peg would have her bed in their stone-flagged kitchen, so that at such times they would merely take up the rugs and all traces could be quickly washed away. So all was well and I believe that Peggy and her new family settled very happily together.

By the time that Solo was expecting her first litter I was getting very worried about Chai. She would not let Solo have any toy but would snatch it away and hide it. You may say she was jealous, and I don't deny that I regarded these two with very different feelings. However I tried to

91

treat them fairly, and being a great believer in the privilege of seniority (at least among dogs) it was Chai who slept on my bed while her junior was relegated to the sitting-room and a chair by the fire.

There was a sliding door between these two rooms, and every morning I would be awakened by horrendous growls. Solo would have come in to say good morning, and Chai would have slipped off the bed and be holding her by standing rigid in every nerve and muscle with her neck curved stiffly over the back of Solo's neck.

If I had spoken sharply or attempted to break this alarming pose manually I believe Solo would have died there and then any morning. Instead I used to slip quietly out of bed on the other side, pretend I hadn't noticed what was going on, and say something casually to attract Chai's attention with my back turned to her.

This broke the tension and enabled her to feel that she had really shown Solo who was boss without being either noticed or punished, and she would release her hold and come to see what was doing.

I took Solo to the vet for a check-up, leaving Chai outside in the car. While in there I told him about these recent developments and he told me to bring her in there and then and let him put her down. As he said, it was better to do it then before Chai did any real damage rather than afterwards since there was no telling what that damage might be. He also gave it as his opinion that if Solo whelped, Chai was capable of killing both her and the puppies.

I believed this because I knew Chai to be a natural killer. She had nearly killed a little Jack Russell bitch in the park, again without any provocation, after which I had never let her off the lead again, thus robbing her of her last source of real enjoyment – a free run.

She had also accounted for several of my ducks by simply biting their heads clean off at the neck. Usually an abnormally quiet and self-contained dog, when she went into action something seemed to snap and she became murderous. At these times she moved with the speed of light. Any rabbit that she saw was as good as dead. She would zoom across the grass like a jet plane and finish the unfortunate rabbit instantly by snapping its backbone in the act of catching it. You never took anything alive out of Chai's mouth.

Now it was all over before I realised what was happening. I couldn't have taken her in cold blood, but in spite of the usual shock and self-recrimination I knew the vet had been right and have always been grateful for the help he gave me that day. Life was certainly a lot easier afterwards.

So now Solo really was my one and only, and it stayed that way for nearly a year. Her first litter, like Peggy's, consisted only of two sons, one of which died at birth. Not liking to leave her alone I took her nearly everywhere with me. She loved the minivan, and in the mirror I could see her with her four feet planted well out so that her little body rode the bumps and curves surely and with ease.

Dogs and cars make an interesting subject. Chai, though never sick, was always far too tense to enjoy a ride, yet one day when I had driven her and Solo to the garage to pick up a new van, she very much surprised me. The old van was an A40, the new one my first minivan, so there was quite a difference in the feel of them.

Having transferred ourselves to the new one I drove into Maidstone where I parked in a side street and got the dogs out to take them to a shop or two. When we were on our way back Chai began sniffing and pulling strongly, apparently in great anxiety. As we came near the van she pulled more strongly than ever, and dragging me to the rear doors began wagging her tail and showing every sign of delighted recognition. I was amazed that she knew it again after so short an acquaintance, and even more surprised at this most un-Chai-like display of pleasure and relief.

Solo surprised me even more one day when I took her into the nearby village to shop. Where I stopped there was plenty of room for cars to park nose to kerb, and while I was relocking I became aware that Solo was making a great kerfuffle round the car beside it. When I looked she was dancing round it on her hind legs, yipping and displaying a lot of excitement.

This puzzled me because the car was empty. Perhaps there was a cat in it? I peered in but there was nothing there. Suddenly the penny dropped. This car was the same model as that owned by the friend who had bred her, a small Renault saloon with the radiator grids situated at the sides in front of the rear wheels.

I often drove over to see this friend and Solo had had ample time to study her car, for it was always parked on the drive in front of mine. Solo adored her breeder, but who would have thought any dog would have memorized a car's details so well, still less that she would be comparing it with other models and be able to say Snap when she spotted its twin?

For there could be no other explanation. It was not engine recognition because the car was stationary and making no noise. Nor was it scent which gave her the clue because this car did not in fact belong to the person she thought it did. To put it beyond doubt I said my friend's name and asked Solo 'You think that's *her* car, don't you?' to which she gave an eager 'yes!' by redoubling her celebrations.

This was something of an eye-opener to me because even those of us who believe dogs do think, tend to assume that their minds are blank unless that are actually doing something, but here was proof of one dog spending her idle hours studying and memorizing the details which distinguish one make and model of car from another, and doing it so well that she was able to identify a similar vehicle when seen suddenly and in quite a different place and context.

I mentioned as proof of Toffee's brain power that she told a lie. So could Solo, and set the scene for it too! The path to the kennels ran beside a long wide flower-bed, and as I had no kitchen garden I had planted an edging of strawberry plants. That year it promised a good crop, yet every time I looked there were lots of fruits ripening but never any ready. I was mystified. No slug trails, no signs of birds pecking. Even after I had marked a number of 'ready tomorrows', when tomorrow came I could see no sign at all of the strawberries, they were just picked clean off their stalks.

One day I was watching Solo from the kitchen window. She trotted quietly out into the garden, holding a red ball in her mouth. As she got to the path beside the strawberries she bounced it once or twice, catching it again, so I was not surprised when it dropped into the row. Her nose went down to retrieve it but didn't come up again. In fact her head had a curious motion suggestive of a horse cropping the grass. So one mystery was solved.

I tapped on the glass and called out 'What do you think *you're* doing?' and had to laugh at the quick, guilty fish-around among the strawberry leaves before the red ball emerged, triumphantly borne in Solo's mouth while her look said innocently 'I was only looking for my ball, I dropped it and it rolled in there.'

Solo loved fruit of all kinds. She would eat blackberries and currants off the bushes, and in late summer could be seen jumping up to pick the purple plums and ripening apples from the lower branches of the trees.

She watched a good deal of television, and unlike most dogs, who are only interested in animals on the small screen, she watched everything. Peggy was an animals-only watcher and once viewed a film in which the action was taken almost entirely by a small boy and a dog. Most of the time the camera swung like a pendulum between the two, giving Peggy an exhausting time. Every time the boy showed up, her head dropped to her paws, only to be jerked up again as soon as Scruffy was back in the picture, rather as if she were watching a tennis match.

I was always puzzled to know how Peggy recognised some of them as animals. She would give about fifty per cent of her usual attention to a horse ridden or pulling a cart, apparently considering the man/horse combination not to be the genuine article. Yet all of her attention was riveted on a picture of a two-toed sloth in a tree: a very bad picture shown on a set somewhat on the blink, the sloth portrayed by an immobile black splodge in the middle of a dark tangle of branches. Then there was the close-up of some weird ants fighting. Peggy could never have seen anything at all like that, yet she was immediately most excited.

There was a very bright little poodle that I once trimmed who loved a series featuring a dog so much that he learnt the signature tune and as soon as he heard it would come rushing in from wherever he happened to be and sit in front of the set to watch 'his' programme. Solo never did that but she reacted to the signature tune of *The Magic Roundabout* just as Scamp did to *Drink to me Only* – by lifting her head from the carpet and howling most dolorously.

Solo watched everything. Mary Whitehouse would have approved of her because she hated violence of any kind on the screen and would dash at it barking in an attempt to make the various cowboys, Indians, soldiers or whatever behave themselves.

She hated programmes with a brooding or ominous theme. One on monsters, fabulous and real, had her curled deep in her chair, bristling and growling, and the telecast of Churchill's funeral gave her a very nasty time. This was an occasion magnificently filmed, but it went on all day. I happened to be at home and kept it going in memory of the magic and comfort of those great wartime speeches coming over the air on gloomy evenings, putting courage, strength and a sense of unity and purpose into us all. It was hard on Solo, she hated the dead marches, the muffled drums, the funereal voices of the commentators.

Solo was for me. She would fetch anything I asked for, and if I lost anything (which I am good at) she would begin looking for it, and if she found it, bark and unmistakably point at it. I have a pathological fear of spiders, and the bungalow was rich in the larger and more athletic kinds. She didn't need to point them out when I was awake, for like many fellow-sufferers I sense the presence of these horrors in a room before I see them. But sometimes she would wake me in the night and I would switch on the light thinking she wanted to go out, but she would quickly turn that suggestion down and stand firmly on point . . . and there it would be on the wall. I would screw myself up to be bloody, bold and resolute and slay the thing. Solo would then relax, I would thank her and we would both go back to sleep. You may think this was a mixed blessing, but it meant never lying awake wondering whether there was a spider there or not. I could take Solo's word for it.

If she did need to go out and I was hard to wake she would simply drag the bedclothes off me!

She never minced matters – if her water bowl was empty she would place it upside down right in the middle of the sitting-room carpet where I couldn't fail to see it. As I used to tell her, I can take a hint if only it's heavy enough.

I had a number of laying ducks which I allowed to roam free in the orchard, only shutting them up at night. Solo was very good with these amiable birds, snow white with pink beaks or in the soft brown uniform of the Khaki Campbell. It didn't take her long to realise that they laid eggs, and she began to collect them and bring them to me, sometimes two at a time. She had a very hard mouth indeed, but strangely she never broke an egg unless she dropped it at my feet on the concrete! She knew that I liked her to bring the eggs and if she ever saw a duck resting on the grass she would gently poke her nose under its tail as if to say 'Come on, give!' It's surprising how often it worked!

Solo was not a very good mother. When she first found herself tied by invisible and unbreakable strings to her first little son, Tiger, she didn't like it at all. Unlike Chai she had no personal animus against him, but was sorely puzzled and repelled by the job of feeding him. Once more I had to hold a puppy to his mother to get his necessary food, but she would stand patiently enough until he was satisfied As she didn't want to stop with him afterwards and he had no company I arranged a well-covered basket for him in an armchair in front of the fire, where he slept contentedly more like a baby than a puppy.

But Solo was obviously very unhappy. I had not expected this, but a little serious thought gave me the answer. She was just shattered because she believed that her intensely happy and carefree life had come to an end. Abruptly she found herself a prisoner, and a prisoner with undreamed-of responsibilities, and she found it traumatic.

I couldn't have that. The day after Tiger was born was bright and sunny. I decided to do a little pruning among the apple trees, and collecting the necessary gear, called Solo. She looked at me as if she couldn't believe her ears. Uncertainly at first, then with the impetuosity of one who has joyfully shrugged off all cares and responsibilities, she followed me to the far end of the orchard.

What a time she had! Rolling in the long green grass, tossing and teasing the red and yellow windfalls from the huge old Bramleys, she was a Solo rejuvenated. For her sake I stuck to the job much longer than I otherwise would, and the bright sunshine had paled and thinned among the trees when I suddenly became aware that something more than play was going on.

Hurriedly descending the ladder I ran to where Solo was rooting at the foot of the hedge which divided my apples from the farmer's pears on the other side. Once at the scene of the crime I was horrified to find she had a hedgehog. With a spade I hurriedly put Prickles over the hedge and into the pears where he belonged, leaving myself with the problem of what to do with Solo. There is nothing like your friendly neighbourhood hedgehog for giving a dog a fan club of considerable membership. And she had a day-old puppy!

She certainly could not go back to him until her new friends were gone, but how to achieve that happy state? I daren't use flea powder for Tiger's sake, and for the same reason didn't fancy an insecticidal shampoo. There was nothing for it but the fine tooth comb, and Solo and I, although both tired, had a busy hour. To my amazement I didn't find a parasite of any kind on her, which I think must have been due to Prickles not having been killed or even much harmed. If he had been dead I think it would have been a very different story, but as it was there were no worse results than a delayed tea for Tiger.

From Solo's point of view it was entirely successful. The happy afternoon's routabout in the orchard had quite restored her faith in the future, and Tiger was now correctly viewed in her mind as a mere interesting incident

98

instead of the end of her youth and good times.

I had been interested in dog Obedience – the sport as opposed to the general principle – for a good many years. Unluckily, although my faith in Airedales kept me obstinately of the opinion that they could be trained as well as any other breed, those I had tried it with were not really starters. I need say no more here about Toffee. Bamu, although willing, was nearly five when she began and, her strength having been sapped by her bad start in life, tired easily. Also her sensitivity, subjected to my early mistakes and clumsiness, made her feel a little in the wrong when I worked her. These two factors made her lag very badly and work with an apologetic air.

Chai decided from the start that training classes were the same kind of hell as dog shows and was a staunch non-co-operator from the word go.

One of the loveliest things that Solo ever did was to present herself to me as my ideal Obedience dog. Her extrovert side enjoyed both training and classes with gusto, while her sensitive side took my teaching seriously and lovingly. It was really a case of just showing her what I wanted. Once understood it was her joy to do it as often as I asked her and as well as she could. Being a fast and confident worker she was much less likely to make the mistakes that had bedevilled Bamu's work.

Unless they have had a similar experience no one can understand the emotion with which I used to stand with Solo sitting correctly at my left side ready for the 'Forward' to commence heelwork. Pride, excitement, love, and above all that sense that with her at my side I was more than equal to all the brickbats Fate could throw at me. And she was an excellent heelworker. Attentive and quite oblivious of anyone else, she trotted neatly at my side. People often remarked on how happy she looked while working. Moreover she was one of those dogs so seldom seen, who at every Halt would not only sit, but place her right paw confidingly on my left foot, thus making lagging impossible. She was placed in almost every competition we entered.

I had a prophetic feeling that she was not going to be a

good breeder, so some time after Tiger had left us I took the opportunity of buying in another puppy, Bamu's granddaughter this time, from the same friend who had bred Solo. I called her Sunshine, or Sunny for short, and no dog was ever better named.

Sunny had some of Bamu's quality of inoffensiveness and Solo loved her from the start, while in her turn Sunny simply transferred her mother-fixation from her dam to this new companion. Strangely enough she grew up to look extremely like Solo, although without the odd ears. She, Solo and Bamu were all of a similar type, small, lively, brightly coloured and combining both the sensitive and the extrovert in their natures.

I always say that you never get the same dog twice, but very rarely it does happen. After I lost Bamu I would have given anything to get another like her and what I got was Chai. In Sunny I did have a second Bamu, extraordinarily like her both physically and mentally, yet it meant less to me than it should have done because, incredibly, I now had something even better. Sunny was a very naughty puppy indeed for the first three weeks, then quite suddenly, as if she had now seen and done everything, she became a reformed character overnight, and the submerged saint began to struggle to the surface.

Solo's second litter again consisted of two puppies, both bitches this time. One became very ill on her second day. After a ten-day struggle during which she did not grow at all, my vet managed to save her with Penbritin, then newly out – in fact it may have been the first time he had used it.

This puppy, later named Socks, was a poor breed specimen and I mentally dismissed her as a future brood. Sally, the other puppy, was much more to my taste and already showed signs of developing her mother's personality. I have never seen a puppy so pleased with her feet! When she first realised their potentialities (at about four weeks) she would run madly about the room, tossing her front legs high so that she could see them, then stop and stand quite still, studying them with an expression of great satisfaction and self-congratulation.

100

But unhappily Sally was also not a prospect for adding to the breeding strength because she was badly parrot-jawed. That is, her bottom jaw extended noticeably beyond her rather short upper one. This is a very bad fault and all mouth faults are difficult to eradicate once introduced into a strain. I could not conscientiously keep her, much as I liked her, so it looked as if I was once again going to be without a daughter of my best beloved dog.

Solo was now just on three so I decided to concentrate on her career in Obedience for a bit while she rested from her maternal duties. One weekend I put her in a local Obedience competition with all the old thrill of taking her into the ring again. She was in the run-off for first place with three others, all with full marks.

They whittled it down till it was just Solo against the last Alsatian. The judge had us doing heelwork up and down, side by side. Both dogs were perfect and at last he threw up his hands in despair. It was my bad luck that he was on our side of the ring and right in Solo's view when he did it. The sudden movement distracted her long enough to cause a late sit and the red rosette went to the Alsatian.

But we had never been in a run-off for first place before and it had been a very close thing. I took it for a good omen for our future success.

I went home feeling very bucked and hopeful, but that night I had a terrible dream that while out with me Solo ran under a bus and was killed. Everyone has had dreams so vivid that they haunt their waking hours. I awoke shattered and depressed, and although I was extra-careful of my darling could not shake off the ominous atmosphere of this dream, which soon proved to be a prophetic one.

Just three days after her triumph at the show Solo got out of the garden in my absence to go rabbiting and was killed on the nearby railway line. She had pushed down one fence restricting her to the garden, gone right to the top of the orchard and climbed another there. It was just another case of what I call 'post-weaning energy surge', for her daughters were just two months old. Also the farmer had been cutting the long grass on his side so she had been able to see the rabbits at play through the wire. It was a lovely day, the first of June, and to her it must have seemed the ideal way to spend it. My only comfort was that she was enjoying life to the end and never suffered a day's illness in her life.

Sunny, then seven months old, was frantic at the loss of her adopted mother and for her sake only I decided to keep Socks after all. If I had two I could leave them at home instead of taking them everywhere with me as I had Solo.

Anyone who thinks I am a fool is probably right. I only knew that for months afterwards I had such a strong feeling of Solo in the car that I used to talk to her as I drove, as if she were really there with me, and as I talked the tears would come. Anyone who saw me pass must have thought I was out of my mind. Why not? I was.

When you lose an old dog it is not so bad even though that dog has become woven into the fabric of your life, for in fact you have already lost so much in him that you once loved. His energy has gone, his playfulness, the sparkle in his eyes. Sleeping the day away he is already almost not here. All these things and many more besides have slipped away from you imperceptibly over the years. When you finally lose what is left of him, it cannot be so great a loss as if it had happened when he was at the crown of his potentialities with hoped-for years to come in which to develop and enjoy them. I have grieved for many dogs, but Solo broke my heart.

Doggy friends were very kind, although not always quite on the spot with their well-meant condolences. They kept telling me that I would forget her in time. I not only didn't want to forget, I hated the thought of forgetting. I was never to see that brave, trim little figure again, but the last thing I wanted was to forget her, and I tried to keep her in my mind as fresh as if I had only seen her yesterday. Again and again I went over my memories, as if by doing so I could force them to stay sharp.

The best thing anyone said to me in this confused and dreary time was that I must think myself lucky ever to have had such a dog, let alone having her to enjoy for three whole years. The friend who said this had had many dogs but freely admitted that she had never had such rapport with any of them as I had experienced with Solo.

Nature never shrinks from the banal or sentimental if it suits her book. There is a weed that grows like bindweed in the Kentish hedgerows. I don't know its name but in late summer it is hung with brilliant scarlet berries. Where Solo had climbed the orchard fence she had broken the plants growing on it away and they were replaced by a swag of this weed. I never noticed it till one day weeks later, when I went into the orchard and saw the splash of it hanging there, a wreath for Solo. It is so vivid in colour that I cannot miss it when I drive round the countryside. Even now, thirteen years later, it takes me by the throat every time.

In the long term the loss of my ideal Airedale was to have some odd effects on me . Although looking after my two puppies helped me more than anything else, they didn't touch my inner self. They were just a couple of puppies to me for a long time. In any case, Socks couldn't have been less like her mother. The only trait she took from her was her one slight imperfection, a tendency to be jealous.

This didn't disappoint me as I hadn't expected a resemblance. Somehow that unlikeness was a perverse satisfaction to me. There could never be another Solo, that I knew, and in a way liked Socks better for not even trying. Later she was found to have a weak heart, probably dating from that early illness and titanic struggle for life when so tiny. I never did breed from her, somehow I didn't want to, and eventually she was spayed.

Poor Tiger had to be put down at an early age. Sally, who had been trained to the gun, did well in spite of her bad mouth, and seems to have been appreciated as much by her owner as Solo was by me. It is terrible to have to report that she was killed by an incompetent vet who went through an artery while spaying her and then sent her home as fit, where she haemorrhaged and died.

It seems a sad and too-early end to Solo's line, but how could that miraculous combination of genes ever recur? No doubt they still exist, scattered throughout the Airedale breed. If ever some of them come together in one dog its lucky owners must say 'what a wonderful dog', but even if they *all* combined it would be a pretty long chance if that lucky owner were to be myself.

There is a saying among dog folk to the effect that you only have one dog, meaning that there will only be one in each life which will be supremely satisfying to your needs, and beside which all others will be found wanting. I once thought mine was Scamp, then later surely it must be Bamu? But it was neither, it was Solo, my little one who was with me for so short a time. This may surprise even some of my closest friends, for I have never been able to talk about her since that terrible day, and after all these years I don't suppose I ever shall.

Villainy reads better than virtue and no doubt Toffee makes a bigger impression on paper, but one loves what one lives with. Of course Sunny and Socks came to mean more to me as time went by, especially my little Bamu-come-back, Sunny. All my present Airedales are descended from her and give me an absorbing interest and great happiness. I have five of them, yet all five together don't give me as much as I got from Solo.

When she died something in me died, and I am still trying to come to terms with the fact that my One Dog is gone.

PART TWO
Trimming

Let the little dogs play,
Unhampered by the felted bands that cling,
Matted and knotted round their prisoned limbs.
Let the little dogs play.

Let the little dogs bark,
Gaily, without the following flinching shake
Of ears deep-fouled by poison and neglect.
Let the little dogs bark.

Let the little dogs dance
On paws ungalled by stones of knife-like mud,
Uncrippled too by nests of curling claws.
Let the little dogs dance.

Let the little dogs boast
Of conscious beauty that must be admired,
And swagger bravely in new-laundered state.
Let the little dogs boast.

Let the little dogs sleep
At ease, in comfort and well-being curled,
And all their dreams be happiness and love.
Let the little dogs sleep.

9
Trial and error

My father had given me Scamp for my thirteenth birth-day, and I was still some weeks short of my fourteenth when the problem of getting him stripped first came up. I flatly refused to let him go away to be done – the horrid shock of finding Jim in his blue elephant bristle after being scalped had made an indelible mark on my mind. Also Scamp did not take too kindly to strangers, and I was afraid that an unsympathetic handler might get bitten and then my hero would be branded as a dangerous and unreliable dog. I declared my intention of doing him myself.

I daresay Dad was short of the price of a professional trim, anyway he gave a very non-committal consent to this plan, the inference being that if I made a mess of the job the whole thing would be taken out of my hands and an expert called in to put it right.

I was thrilled, and set to work. The only tools I had were an old coarse steel comb and a pair of cheap scissors. I don't know where I got the latter – probably they were an old pair discarded by my elder sister whose hobby was dressmaking.

A terrier with a wiry coat should have it plucked – literally pulled out by the roots. This is the correct definition of the word 'stripped' in this connection. I believe I did know this in theory but not for one moment did I propose to go about the job in this way. For a start I had no idea how it was done. If I had known, I did not possess the necessary tools, and if I had possessed them I wouldn't have known how to use them. No, my own hair was always cut with scissors and I don't think it ever crossed my mind to use any other method on the dog.

So I set to work. Young as he was, Scamp was always compliant, so my way was free of at least one rock on which I might have floundered. Sitting on a sheet of newspaper with him in the back yard, private from inquisitive eyes and sarcastic tongues, I began chopping manfully away and soon a great deal of loose hair was blowing around. I found it quite hard work and laid the foundations of some lifelong blisters on my fingers, but it was so absorbing to see a brand new shape emerging from the woolly clouds.

When I stepped back to take a look I wasn't ill-pleased with the general effect but rather shaken to see that my dog was covered in hundreds of 'rat bites' or scissor marks. I wasn't going to let Dad see him like that, so I set to again to get rid of them by clipping each big mark away with half a dozen little cuts, rather on the macadamizing principle which makes a smooth road from many tiny stones. While doing this I made my first discovery – that the worst rat bites are produced by cutting across the hair and that marks are much less if the scissor blades are held parallel to the direction of growth when cutting.

I know I didn't shape his legs properly, left him with a bustle at the rear and probably made a sloppy job of his head and neck. Nevertheless I felt elated, and when Dad, rising from his afternoon nap and coming out with the expected demand 'let's see the damage' gave a grudging 'Not bad', I was fit to burst with pride. Scamp was delighted too, he felt cool and comfortable and off we went to the Park to show off. Of course, all the time I looked at him and looked at him, checking my work, and making mental notes, and in the next week or two I considerably improved on it. I made my second discovery, that combing the hair the wrong way showed up the rough cutting so that I could more easily even it out. I also began comparing Scamp's trim with pictures in the few dog books I could get hold of, and corrected many mistakes in this way. Scamp began to look quite smart, and several neighbours and relations made approving comments on his appearance.

And so was born my Great Idea. The long summer holiday was just beginning and I had time on my hands. I would undertake (for a very small fee) to do a similar service for any other lucky dog owner who might desire it. I always liked killing two birds with one stone, and if all went well I saw nothing to stop me learning this all-absorbing new art on such convenient dogs and at the same time augmenting my scanty pocket money. This latter ambition was always with me, but previous projects had always come to grief if not actual disaster. Was I, by the benign genius of The Dog, on to a winner at last? Probably not, but at least I knew I was going to enjoy trying.

Naturally I consulted my mother first, rather fearing that she would veto the idea, but she had great faith in all her children and always encouraged us whenever possible and I well remember her stout 'Others can do it, why not you?'

It was all I needed. Nowadays such a child, inspired with such an ambition, would surely be given at least a little adult guidance in where to find information and know-how, and would not only be helped with the purchase of a basic toolkit but would expect and indeed demand it. But at that time I'm sure this never occurred to either of us, certainly I had no such expectations, and my comb and scissors quite filled my idea of the necessary equipment. In fact I can remember a feeling of satisfaction in their very simplicity, for it meant that if all came to nothing there could be no financial crash and consequently no one could reproach me. When you start at the bottom you can't fall, and I rejoiced that I had all to gain and nothing to lose.

After trimming Scamp, of course, those old scissors were awfully blunt, especially as I didn't hesitate to use them for any other purpose that arose. I actually had to learn at first hand that scissors lose their edge by use, and only acquired this item of knowledge after blistering every finger of my right hand in a big way. I'm not sure what my remedy was for this problem. Old Knives-to-grind came down our street quite often with his grindstone mounted on an old sewing-machine treadle and carried in a little handcart, but I fancy it was my father who tried to service my scissors by applying their blades briskly to the back doorstep. This couldn't have been very successful, because I know I began to study the ironmonger's windows and at intervals to buy new scissors from my earnings.

I didn't wait for work to come to me. Looking round for suitable victims I picked on an Airedale dog who had a job as guard at a builder's yard across the street, and, inwardly quaking if outwardly bold, went and asked if I might trim him. I remember that his name was Pat and that he was a young dog and very sweet. For this second scissor-and-comb job I had the nerve to ask for half a crown, and very thrilled I was to get it, for it was more than double my weekly pocket money.

My next job was a friend's wire haired terrier, and here I received a setback, for Chummy belied his name and objected to the process so strongly that my friend's mother stepped in and forbade me to go on because she was afraid I would be bitten. I was most indignant, also disappointed, because I viewed this snapping little beast in the light of both a challenge and a stepping-stone in my education. She offered me a shilling, which I refused, and which my mother said I should have taken.

However, I had the bit between my teeth, and continued my studies, charging very reasonable rates indeed. Coming from a background coloured always by what we called 'chronic shortness' the earnings of these shillings and half-crowns meant a lot to me, while I felt that my ridiculously low prices protected me from any owner enraged by my unwittingly spoiling his dog's beauty. Not that I ever had any complaints – even if I seldom had repeat orders. I was still only thirteen, which I suppose was sufficient caveat to my customers.

In between 'jobs' I spent my spare time roaming Southwark Park with Scamp. I talked to all the dog owners and got to know every dog by its name and breed, and nothing thrilled me as much as seeing an unusual specimen. Dogs were very different in the early thirties, wire haired fox terriers were top of the pops but already foreshadowing their own decline with the extreme unreliability of the over-popular dog.

Among big dogs Airedales were high in popularity. Alsatians were scarce, Labradors almost unknown, at least in town, and boxers hardly to be met with even in the pages of a book. One could see a few collies, pekes, poms, Scotties, cairns, spaniels and golden or flat-coated retrievers. One Old English sheepdog and one rarely seen Irish wolfhound occasionally frequented the park, but few people had ever heard of the Afghan hound, Pyrenean, Westie, Dobermann or many others of today's most numerous varieties. Terriers were probably the most favoured group, with smooth fox terriers, Manchesters and even Bedlingtons quite often kept even in town: three breeds not often met with anywhere today. What would be more unusual now – to walk down the street with an Afghan hound or one of these? Such is fashion.

However, no thought of all this troubled my infant enthusiasm. Hutchinson's Dog Encyclopaedia began to come out in weekly parts, and with the help of my sister Nell I acquired every one, poring over it devoutly each week and awaiting the next issue impatiently, eager to learn what hitherto unknown breed would grace its pages. I didn't realise that my studies, theoretical and practical, were the beginnings of a long road leading at last to a career with dogs. How pleased I would have been if I had known – I might even have been able to take a few short cuts to that goal.

After we had moved to Petts Wood and while I was still

111

at school I decided to try my luck with a card in a shop window. Luck was right, for the shopman, after reading my carefully written card and staring at me very hard, said I could leave it in for as long as I liked but refused to take any money for it. This was perhaps just as well as I didn't get many replies, largely because in those days – what we might call the pre-poodle age – it was very much less common for owners to have their dogs trimmed at all, and poodle parlours were virtually non-existent. All the same, I made out my card with immense pride, sketching the lettering in lightly first in pencil and then going over it in Indian ink so that it wouldn't fade in the shop window. One quarter of it was always occupied by a highly simplified and stylised picture of a wire haired terrier, obviously very smartly trimmed. I chose a wire in preference to an Airedale partly because so many people had them and partly because one or two well placed black patches made them look so showy in pen and ink.

The first customer I obtained through my card was a charming Scotswoman who brought her Scottie and sat and chatted while I worked. I went to her house for subsequent trims and continued to attend little Judy for many years to the end of her life, and her mistress recommended me to several others. I must have been improving! Of course I had my setbacks, as with the little wire bitch who went berserk on the departure of the two young women who left her and had to be returned to them in the same state in which she had arrived.

Once I answered the door to a man who turned out to be the secretary of the local country club wanting me to sign a contract to do the dogs belonging to his members. He was confused to say the least when he realised that this gym-slipped apparition was the expert he had come to interview. Needless to say I was game, or perhaps reckless would be a better word, but my mother put her foot down and the poor man was able to make his escape.

Another memorable call was from a lady who was returning to India with a pair of show wires and wanted them hand-stripped before leaving for the hot climate. She was equally surprised when she saw me, and as I frankly admitted that hand-stripping was an art I did not possess I thought she too would retreat. But being as I suppose an Empire-builder she was made of sterner stuff, and said that if I was willing to do the work she would show me how it was done. In this way I made my first acquaintance with a stripping comb and learnt how to use it. I also noticed how different these show wires were from the pet specimens I had learnt to dread. They looked different, their coats were different, and how their behaviour was different! They were a dog and bitch and I remember their names to this day – Copenhagen Storm and Copenhagen Cloud. I wonder if anyone else would know those names now?

I found hand trimming very hard work and can't say I used it much after this job was done. I never even tried it on Scamp, which was a pity as it would have improved his looks considerably. But somehow I never quite forgot it, and later on found it came more easily. With the advent of my lovely little Bamu I decided to give it a try, and she was the first of my dogs to be properly stripped. The improvement was so obvious that I decided it was a must for my own dogs at least, and as time went on began to use it more and more for others too and eventually it became a valuable part of my stock-in-trade.

10

A Toe In the Water

In spite of the early passion with which I embraced my chosen study, and in spite of their usual readiness to encourage lawful enthusiasms, my parents flatly refused to let me become a kennelmaid, which was the only pathway I could see to my longed-for elysium of a career in dogs.

Although I believed, and still believe, that they were mistaken in this, it is not difficult to understand their motives. They lived in a tightly closed and intensely parochial society. Work to them really meant doing things that other members of the family had done. If male they most likely worked in the fish market. My own father was a Billingsgate porter and proud of it, as were many of his family. Even Uncle George's job 'in printing' was spoken of with some awe as if on another plane, although we all knew that due to his injury and disability he did hardly any actual work but idled his days away happily enough in the protection of his mates and union. I also had two grown up boy cousins who hired a barrow and set up a green-grocery stall in the local market. This was regarded as very enterprising and a great leap in the dark, although I believe they did very well with it.

My mother had had a short spell 'in service' and was quite clear that no daughter of hers was going to follow suit. She was very set on us all being 'taught a trade'. This was no good to me as for a girl it meant going to the Borough Polytechnic and learning some branch of the rag trade. Both of my sisters went there. May, the elder, became a very talented dressmaker and also worked as a machine embroideress, while Nell excelled in the latter skill.

It was perhaps fortunate for me that the gap in ages gave me time to see how Nell, at least, suffered in health and spirits by her bondage to this form of slavery in the sweat-shops. Also I didn't have the patience or application of my seniors, and governed probably more by instinct than reason, vetoed this line of country very decisively.

However I was no nearer the kennels. The trouble was that nowhere among all our circle of relatives could be found anyone with any doggy experience or contact at all, only the greengrocer cousins who had gone in for racing greyhounds in a small way. But racing greyhounds weren't at all what I wanted. I had formed a poor opinion of them from seeing them walked in groups of four or five by the local layabouts for a small stipend. They looked skinny and spiritless to me and yet had been known to kill more than one small dog if accidentally let slip in the park. I felt they were the complete opposite to Scamp, my hero.

I remember confiding my ambition to a young woman who used to walk her dog at the same time as myself. She advised me strongly to give it up. Her sister had been a kennelmaid, she said. She had been treated worse than a dog, worked hard seven days a week for a few shillings, been given all the filthiest jobs and hardly enough food to keep her alive. I can't deny that this report discouraged me, but I still cherished the secret belief that not all kennels could be that bad. But how to find a good one? I simply had no idea, and then it would have meant leaving home, which I was loth to do.

Also, I was reputed to be 'bright'. Had I not won a scholarship (just)? And in virtue of this wasn't I installed as a pupil of the local grammar school? Having bought my new uniform at some sacrifice to themselves by parents were entitled to think I should 'better myself'. That meant I should get an office job, and on consideration I thought so too.

So I left school after some years of alternating happiness and boredom. Most of my teachers had been mediocre, some diabolical and just two or three brilliant. With my final exam results better than any of them had expected, I think all except these last two or three breathed a sigh of relief to see me heading out of their lives and into the Civil Service, a square peg in a round hole if ever there was one.

Why had I opted for the Civil Service? Because the hours were short and the holidays comparatively long, and thus I would ensure the maximum time to be out with Scamp or even to continue with my still all-absorbing hobby of trimming! Not surprisingly I made a pretty awful Civil Servant. Before long my blotter and memo pads were covered with sketches of dogs. I would become interested in one particular breed and draw nothing else for weeks until I felt I really knew it in type, character and conformation. I tried to suggest the texture of its coat. A lot of honest effort went into this activity and I barely noticed my superior officers' resentment of it, much as I had been used to infuriate my teachers by enlivening all my question papers with borders of variegated canines.

When I was not drawing or day-dreaming I was very unhappy, yet this period was not without its lighter side. The three girls who were my closest colleagues were great fun, with terrific senses of humour, and we became a sort of Four Musketeers. When they discovered that I had a knack for writing humorous verses my talents became in great demand for 'poems' to give their boy friends commenting on various incidents in their love lives. Even more popular were the gems I occasionally perpetrated

116

about the office personnel, which achieved quite a large circulation. I regret to say that although I played dumb I was well aware that the office bosses also read these efforts and regarded them with an uneasy mixture of amusement and exasperation. But the constant demand for 'a poem' became a burden as it interfered with my day-dreaming, and eventually I had to cut down production in self defence. Work, you will notice, came a bad third.

Two years after I started work the war began, and for me that was a strange muddled time of fear and fun. Although I lived fifteen miles from work I made it a point of honour to turn up whenever humanly possible in spite of air raids and chaotic train services. I was even congratulated by my superiors for this – it was a pity I wasn't more use when I got there. The basement had been converted into an air raid shelter and I seemed to spend a lot of time down there.

Part of the shelter had been commandeered by the Forestry Commission for storage and I used to read the romantic names of the great trees on the cabinets and be away in dreams until I could smell the scent of the pines, feel the slippery carpet of needles under my feet and see Scamp bounding jack-rabbit among the bracken. One thing I learned was that the poet who wrote that stone walls do not a prison make wasn't wrong. Returning reluctantly to reality with the sound of the All Clear I would ask myself why on earth I was wasting away my life filing advice notes.

Fortunately for all concerned my clerical career was cut short by my getting married at the age of twenty. At that time it was still the rule that a female Civil Servant had to give up her job on marriage, and I certainly wasn't arguing.

I still had a few trimming customers at the beginning of the war, including the Scotswoman with her Scottie, and I remember with affection the elderly fellow-clerk who, consulted as to suitable wording for some new window cards which I was roughing out in office time, gravely suggested 'Dogs trimmed by the day, job or hour'. However, dogs were at a discount during hostilities, many were put down, or if they died were not replaced, and few families had any cash to spare for beautifying the dog if they did have one. Feeding a dog became more and more difficult as the stringencies of rationing made the scrap-plate a thing of the past, and Airedales in particular, because of their size, were steadily disappearing.

So, although I would have been glad of any extra money as our weekly income was very narrow indeed in these years, apart from a few old faithfuls trimming jobs were thin on the ground. Still rejoicing in my release from bondage I decided that as one couldn't go anywhere or do very much while the war lasted, it would be sound planning if I devoted what remained of it to the job of producing a family. This I did, and my second baby was some months old by VE day.

There was a tremendous boom in pedigree dogs after the war, combined with an influx of breeds previously unknown or not very often seen. In the vanguard were cocker spaniels, closely followed by Labradors, golden retrievers, Alsatians and boxers. Terriers of all kinds suffered a decline.

When I acquired Jane, my cocker, I was naturally interested in keeping her nice, and since she was a good specimen I learnt the correct method of hand trimming that breed. A trimmed cocker was very smart in those days. To me it is a tragedy that the craze for 'furnishings' in the showring led to breeding for more and more profuse coats, destroying the sleek silky texture and crisp sturdy outline of these beautiful dogs.

With all these good dogs about there was naturally more interest in keeping them looking as they should, but unfortunately for me most of them carried non-trim coats and it still hadn't occurred to me that I had a potential source of income literally in my hands. Two things changed all that, the advent of my little Bamu and the arrival of the miniature poodle.

From Bamu I really learnt the art of hand-stripping, and as I began to sell her puppies, and later Toffee's, I gradually acquired a small nucleus of customers for hand trimming. Owing to the hard work involved it has always been difficult to get this particular job done properly, so providing I gave reasonable satisfaction these dogs would in most cases be customers for life.

However, it was the sudden flood of poodles which actually set the whole thing going in a big way. For the first time the man in the street really began looking at his dog and seeing the state its coat was in. Poodle parlours sprang up everywhere. Very bad a lot of them were, but they did a brisk trade and not only in poodles – owners of other breeds wanted their dogs kept tidy too. I heard rumours of husband and wife teams actually giving up *jobs* to go into this new trade and making greatly increased incomes from it.

It took my breath away, but how could I jump on the bandwaggon? My husband was not at all doggy, and looking after my home and family took all my time and energy as I was not much more gifted domestically than I had been as a Civil Servant. Also I had no electric clippers, couldn't afford to buy any and wouldn't have known how to use them if I had. Nor was there any money to spare for me to take a course. Regretfully I excluded poodles from my list of breeds I could trim.

Then one day I had a phone call from a woman who wanted me to trim her poodle. I explained my difficulties but she didn't care. Her dog had come home from the parlour terrified and bleeding and she refused to let it go there again. She had heard I trimmed dogs at home and was quite ready to accept a scissor trim to achieve this. As for styling, she herself would tell me how the dog should be cut.

This was more than I could resist, so I agreed. I was pretty good with the scissors by now and soon had Mitzi looking quite presentable, and her owner was pleased. I read a few books and kept my eyes sharply on the proliferating poodles around me, comparing, evaluating and criticising their coiffures. At last I felt I must get some clippers and bought a pair out of the proceeds of one of Toffee's litters. I got the make recommended by one of the books, and twenty-odd years later I still use the same model, although I am now on my third pair!

I was now equipped, but felt very nervous about actually using my new weapon as I had never even seen clippers in action. Eventually I contacted Mitzi's owner and offered a free trim in exchange for the opportunity to use them on her dog. I also offered half-price trims for the rest of Mitzi's life. As always when I enter on this kind of contract this was all Mitzi needed to be assured of more than her allotted span. She was seventeen before she eventually handed in her dinner bowl!

My clientele steadily increased, so that when the final break-up of my marriage confronted me, after twenty years, with the necessity of earning my own keep I found that I had, almost without realising it, followed my mother's precept and 'learnt a trade'. I had had my toe in the water for a long time and found it warm and inviting. I now plunged in with high hopes and a deep sense of satisfaction.

At last I had a career in dogs.

11

The Two-Legged Element

One effect of the poodle boom was that I soon found it unnecessary to renew my shop-window cards advertising my service.

Poodle parlours were popping up all over the place, but unfortunately many of them seemed to be staffed by people with little feeling for the job and less for the dogs . . . 'Anything goes' seemed to be their motto, and they often treated their human customers with a high-handedness that took my breath away: as when a lady defended her choice of comb against the one the proprietor wanted her to buy, on the grounds that it was like the one her mother used on her poodles, and was told 'if your mother combs her dogs with a comb like that they must look a mess!'

I began to get a steady stream of ex-parlour customers and soon knew by repute which parlours were good and which were torture chambers. These dissatisfied customers usually chose me because I was willing to work in their homes, where they could step in and forcibly restrain me from committing mayhem on their pets. I had a lot of very difficult trims at that time because naturally it is the dog which has been hurt or terrified previously which is going to be the hardest to cope with.

One was a ten-month-old puppy only trimmed once before, when she had one side of her skull completely skinned and been returned raw, bleeding and in a state of shock, with the advice that she be put down as incurably vicious. She had been under the vet for months after this incident. Naturally she was paralytic with terror when I turned up, but luckily I am naturally patient with dogs and she eventually became very fond of me. She certainly never showed the slightest sign of vice.

Since I've been trimming I have heard a good many horror stories – a dog with the skin supporting the penis partly shorn through, another with a broken jaw and three teeth knocked out, an adorable Sealyham puppy returned with a badly damaged eye and her nature so changed that before long she had to be destroyed as unsafe. My advice to anyone looking for a trimmer is to stop the owner of any well-trimmed dog and ask where it was done. Ask as many people as you can – if you get several good recommendations to the same place your dog will be safe. There are lots of very good and kind trimmers, but they are unlikely to be advertising; they can get all the work they can handle without that.

I have always enjoyed doing a variety of dogs and this naturally brought more grist to my mill, for in those days many parlours refused to trim anything but poodles. I suspect their somewhat sketchy 'training' didn't cover other breeds and coats. Some refused to do mongrels, accepting only pedigree dogs and clipping them all as if they were poodles. Many a terrier has been returned to its bewildered owner with bare feet, shaggy ears and rudimentary topknot and tail pom!

I just couldn't understand how anyone with pretensions to expertise could accept a dog for trimming without so much as a glance at a picture to check up on the correct style for the breed. The fact was that there were a lot of clipper-happy 'cowboys' who thought they had struck a rich vein of easy money. They hadn't. Trimming dogs is very hard work, often dirty and sometimes disgusting. I can't recommend it to anyone unless they have that obstinate yen for dogs that makes working with them a privilege and pleasure sufficient to compensate for the drawbacks of the job.

However, the inevitable swing of fashion at last resulted in a big reduction in the poodle population, and these bad parlours were the first to feel the pinch and shut up shop. The remaining establishments also took more interest in the other breeds, and although it is still extremely difficult to find anyone who will hand-strip a terrier or even a spaniel, the general level of work and handling has very much improved on those early days.

Personally I have never felt any wish for a parlour of my own. I believed that small was safe, and although my trimming equipment was now considerably more than the original comb and scissors, still I felt that to open a shop would be a leap forward so much bigger than any I had taken before that a horrid crash must result. I preferred to visit my dogs, and with the acquisition of a car and a driving licence I was more than content.

A new element, all unlooked for, was also creeping in. I found myself becoming increasingly interested in my human customers. They were so varied, and so were their homes. From caravan to stately home, I've visited them all, and from penurious pensioner to millionaire, my job has given me a sort of bird's-eye view of humanity – at least as it manifests itself in south-east England. Considering that they all have one thing in common – a dog in need of a trim – my random selection is really astonishingly comprehensive.

I soon found that my pleasure or otherwise in a projected call had little to do with the dog but depended almost entirely on the human customer concerned. Some are so friendly, so appreciative of my efforts and seem to enjoy my visits so much, that their appointments are more like social occasions than jobs of work.

I suppose anyone who lives alone sometimes needs

help or advice. In my case there always seems to be customer there to give it. For instance, when I had to go to hospital for an operation it was a customer who drove me there and another who picked me up afterwards and brought me home.

When on the verge of a particularly difficult removal another customer sent her husband, a remarkably tough septuagenarian, to dismantle my kennel fences for transport to my new address. For weeks he worked through wintry weather, bare armed, for two hours every day until they were all done.

On my arrival in my new house I sank down exhausted among my heaped up effects, with harrowed dogs stalking restlessly around me looking for non-existent beds. It was nearly dark, I couldn't find anything, I was tired past the point of being able to think clearly and I wished I was dead.

Came a knock on the door. A customer in the next village had sent round her husband, and there he stood, hands full of flowers and a welcome-to-your-new-home card, asking if there was anything he could get me or do for me. I fear I was incoherent, but somehow he understood, and soon came back bearing a torch, a light bulb, a box of matches for the fire, a kettle, a bar of soap and some sandwiches. He hauled a discarded box-spring in from the garden on which the three dogs promptly flopped, groaning with relief. He then passed into the night and out of my life. To all these and many many more I will always be grateful.

At the other end of the scale are the customers I dread visiting. One pathetic old lady had a really revolting husband who was often around the house when I called. He was bald, inebriate, cross-eyed, with black and broken teeth and a strong tendency to dribble, yet incredibly on one of my visits his wife sat and cried to me because he had left her for a younger woman! He was then seventy-five! I was torn between amazement that any younger woman (or older either) could possibly want him, and astonishment that his wife wasn't overjoyed to see him go. Unfortunately the prodigal returned at the end of the week with all his objectionable qualities undimmed, including his habit of telling me just how Nellie should be clipped. All this I could have borne for the old lady's sake. What I really found hard to take was the state of poor Nellie herself, invariably filthy, matted and with ears crackling with stinking black wax.

Yet strange to say she had so strong a love-fixation for this decrepit old object that his mere presence in the house was enough to set her wailing and struggling to get off the table to be with him, until I could cheerfully have strangled her. Love certainly is a rum thing, and in this case at least proves that dogs aren't nearly as selective as is popularly believed.

The important thing to remember about dog lovers is that they are divided into two camps, the doggy and the pet people. These terms originated with the doggy people, and they use the second with a certain condescension, for between these two factions there exists a mutual suspicion and distrust.

Pet people tend to regard the doggy with some awe as the possessors of a certain mystique. This unfortunately makes them push-overs for the unscrupulous among the fraternity. Just after the war I met a couple who had just paid thirty pounds for an Alsatian puppy. This was a very high price in those days. They told me they didn't have the pedigree because that would have cost a further hundred pounds and they only wanted the dog! It seems incredible that even the most ingenuous of pet people should swallow this, but you see they thought the breeder must be an authority on all such points. And much more recently I saw a cream cross-bred Labrador which had been bought at a greatly inflated price as a pure-bred long-coated white Alsatian. The innocent owners had no idea that both coat and colour were disqualifications under the breed standard, and that the 'rarity' for which they had paid so dear consisted mostly in finding both faults in one animal.

It is this sort of thing, followed by the realisation that they have been done which gives rise to the distrust felt by pet people. Not for nothing has the English language been enriched by the expression 'sold a pup'.

Pet buyers can be very irritating to doggy people by their habit of expressing their dislike of pedigree breeding accompanied by the determination to have 'a good one'. They particularly distrust inbreeding without having for the most part a very clear idea of what it is all about, and their only criterion of a good pedigree is that it is 'as long as your arm', which is apparently the statutory length.

Some take these feelings to the extreme of insisting on a Good Old Mongrel, which to hear them talk seems to be assured of perfection by the haphazard nature of its conception.

While waiting in the vet's one day with three of my Airedales, I chatted with a middle-aged lady who was also waiting. She told me proudly that she had a Good Old Mongrel, her fourth, and 'wouldn't have any other breed' – her very words – as pure-bred dogs had so much wrong with them owing to the evil machination of the breeders. To my amusement she went on to say that her present pet had to be kept permanently sedated owing to a chronic hysterical condition. She was waiting then to give the vet a report and get more tablets – Beauty was much too nervous and snappy to attend in person. With a perplexed sigh she added that all her previous dogs had been the same and she didn't know why she should have such bad luck with them.

Such a coincidence could only have been her fault in some way, but I'm afraid I couldn't resist the temptation to say solemnly 'Ah, it's in the breed!' My turn to go into the surgery coming at this opportune moment, I didn't have a chance to see the result of this remark, but I hope it gave her food for thought. It never seems to occur to the Good Old Mongrel fans that their animals have been selectively bred for at least one quality – a propensity to roam. Still less that they may very well have been inbred to an extent which would give a bona fide breeder the cold horrors. I personally have known of two cases where the same dog was not only the father of most of the local mongrels, but also their grandfather and sometimes great grandfather as well. Not surprisingly these offspring were

126

often extremely unreliable in temperament, some really suffering from advanced nervous instability.

Misconceptions such as these form part of the basis for the antagonism which doggy people have for pet people. For with all their faults they do have an involvement with dogs which makes it hard for them to suffer fools gladly, when such foolishness so often rebounds upon the dog.

Doggy people usually have an objective and realistic view of dogs; pet people too often see them as little idealised humans. So much so that one sometimes can't help thinking that Mummy might go off Paddy with the speed of light if she knew what he was really after sometimes when being so cute.

Dogs can be pretty fundamental but many owners prefer to ignore this baser side altogether. Like the woman who always asked me to leave plenty of hair on her dog's rear elevation as 'I don't like to see his little arrangements!' Another lady rang to ask if I would postpone her poodle's trim as 'she – well – that is to say – I'm afraid she's become *unwell.*' I replied cheerfully that I didn't mind in the least and would prefer to do the trim on the specified date. This confused her a little but she rallied strongly with the remark 'Oh well, I don't suppose it will matter because she's wearing knickers and I expect you can get plenty off the rest of her.' Needless to say Poppy's panties came off as soon as I got my hands on her and I returned her and them separately with the brutal advice to rely on chlorophyll tablets and give the bitch a chance to clean herself.

A customer once told me, with a chuckle at her own idiocy, how she had once had a dear little mongrel who had a special sweetheart in the same road. This little dog was so faithful and persistent that at last he melted the lady's already soft heart. She opened the door wide, saying kindly, 'If you love her so much you'd better come in and see her.' And was astounded by ensuing events. Old Faithful must have thought it too good to be true, and the loving couple were enriched in due course by six bonny babies. My customer had never thought her little Lucy was that kind of girl!

In spite of these mutual antipathies, however, pet owners and doggy people need and depend on each other. The pet owner needs the breeder to supply his puppy, and seldom realises the debt he owes him for his care of the breed in question. The breeder needs the pet owner, for without him there would be no pet market where he could dispose of his surplus puppies, and without this he could not continue to breed. This arrangement generally speaking, works well: in fact I often think that this country's acknowledged superiority in the production of high quality dogs may well owe a great deal to the support which its pet buyers give to the breeder in buying and demanding sound, good looking dogs, thereby helping them to keep up the standard of their stock.

12
Case Book

I have now been trimming for well over forty years, and it is only to be expected that during that time I have come across some odd and funny things in the process. Here are a few that come to mind.

I have had at least one millionaire on my books, and of all my customers he was the only one that I really had difficulty in getting my money from. I never saw him, because he engaged me by telephone, and as he was in London getting richer still all the week I always dealt with his housekeeper when I went to collect the dog from his gem of an Elizabethan manor house. This was far and away the most beautiful house I ever visited on my rounds, at least from the outside. When I went in I never got further than the kitchen, and that was furnished with a poverty and meanness that made me sorry for the poor woman.

She was always in a terrible state when I came to collect my fee. She wanted me to send in a bill and wait for a cheque by post. Since nobody else had ever suggested this procedure I saw no point in starting it then, it seemed so silly. She always paid me, but since she did not speak English very well I couldn't understand her evident distress until I arrived one day and found that she had been posted to the London house and been replaced by another who explained the situation.

It seemed that when His Lordship decamped for London on Monday mornings he left her no money at all to run the house. Tradesmen and everyone else were paid by cheque. Apparently I had been the only rebel, and the housekeeper's agony was caused by the fact that owing to my low insistence on cash on the nail she was having to pay me out of her own pocket and then having the utmost difficulty in extracting it from her master's coffers.

Why did she bother? I would then have bid them farewell and it would have been back to the poodle parlour for the dog. This was what she feared, because until I had turned up with my obliging collection and delivery service she and her husband had had the job of escorting it to its barber in a town twenty miles off – and they had to do this on their day off!

When I was a child I had a fantasy that one day I would help an old lady across the road and that she would subsequently leave me all her gold. Somehow things have never turned out this way. For many years I trimmed a dog for an elderly widow who lived alone with her charming but rather difficult Sealyham. She was delighted that I could handle Suzy without much trouble and often hailed friends passing by to come in and see Suzy sitting smugly on the table and putting up obligingly with her quarterly trim.

In the course of our long acquaintance a good many confidences passed on either side. She had no children and had been very happy with her husband and for his sake said she didn't want to leave her large and rather lovely house, which she said cost her far more than she could afford. Always a sucker for the hard luck story I trimmed Suzy for all those years at a price well below the usual rate.

She told me how she hated her few remaining relatives who all lived a long way away and never visited her, and often said how hard things were for women like myself who were all alone and struggling to buy a house and make a living with their bare hands. In spite of all this I never once thought of that childhood fantasy until one day she collapsed and died and I learnt that she had left not only the house but a hundred thousand pounds all to charity! I couldn't help laughing at myself. Goodbye fantasy! But I still think she might have left me a fiver or two, if only to square the account for all those cut price trims!

I'd been going to another customer for some time and had only vaguely noticed her somewhat unusual taste in books when I discovered that she was a medium and highly thought of in local spiritualist circles. She told me that she held seances and other sessions in which, under the influence of her Spirit Guide, she was able to answer questions and give advice to the troubled. Not, I must emphasise, for any financial consideration. She made no charge because she believed that if she did she would lose her powers.

It was impossible to be other than convinced of her sincerity, and I trust she would forgive me a private smile when I heard that she had thrown a rather valuable collection of silver into the dustbin because she thought it was too blackened by neglect to be worth selling. However, perhaps I do her Guide an injustice in thinking that he slipped up in allowing her to do this. It may be that some dustman in deep financial waters was saved by the discovery of this treasure trove. I hope so; I hate to think of the Council's getting it.

Walking into another house one day I found the children entertaining a goat in the sitting-room. Well, you never know what you're going to walk in on; but the goat wasn't nearly so odd as the frog kept by another family in their bath. It was the sole relict of a batch of tadpoles hatched by the son while still at school. They thought it would be cruel to turn it loose like a canary among sparrows, so they accommodated it permanently in the bath, merely giving it a change of scene in a bucket when they wanted to use the bath themselves. Its sole furniture was an upturned plastic bowl under which it sometimes used to sit. They fed it with worms dug from the garden and it was a very fat, prosperous-looking frog in bright green and yellow, although its basilisk eye used to unnerve me rather on the occasions that I used the bathroom myself. He must have been a Methuselah among frogs when he eventually succumbed to the strain of the family moving house.

One woman that I very much admired had a poodle which developed diabetes and subsequently went blind. After learning how to inject insulin she taught the other members of the family in case she was ever prevented from being home at the right time, and set about conquering the problems raised by the dog's loss of sight. She took to carrying a walking-stick when she took her out, and by tapping it on the kerb and telling the dog to sit when a step up or down was indicated, soon got her confidence out of doors again.

Next she tied a bell to the stick, and by this means she was able to give the little dog free exercise as the sound of the bell gave her position. I was most intrigued with these experiments and very much admired my customer's ingenuity and persistence. She deserved a better reward. Unhappily the dog soon had a further breakdown and was put down to save further suffering. This is one owner who need never have any secret self-reproach as to whether she had done all she could for her dog.

The closer families live together the more likely there is to be trouble over dogs or anything else. Shared entries are a notorious cause of trouble. I had a friend who owned a small pug and lived in a house which shared its front path with the one next door. Her neighbours were painfully house-and-garden proud to such an extent that the very geraniums and marigolds were measured to make quite certain they were even.

Puggy was a good little chap and never ran on to the neighbours' front garden when going in and out, but on these occasions Jenny was always conscious of a pair of gimlet eyes behind the lace curtains waiting for a false step.

132

As Jenny herself was not the most placid of mortals it is not surprising that the flare-up, when it came, was a notable one.

It happened one day when Jenny was in a hurry and Puggy dashed down the path with an excited bark just as the neighbouring husband was coming up it. Maybe he'd had a bad day at the office, maybe he really thought he was being attacked, but in any case he lashed out at Puggy with his walking-stick and a few nasty words. The stick didn't connect with Puggy's person or anywhere near it, but Puggy, entering into the spirit of the thing, yelped as if every bone in his body had been broken.

That was enough for Jenny. Although she knew he hadn't been touched she promptly went up in flames. Gathering her little dog to her bosom she swept back into the house, where she proceeded to make some artistic marks in red ink on his back.

There was an elderly vet still practising near Jenny, although I fear he should have been put out to grass some years before. His eyesight wasn't too good, and it wasn't difficult to persuade him that Puggy was bearing the marks of a brutal attack. Armed with his certificate to this effect she sued the neighbour and won!

As she said to me afterwards, 'What pleased me was that *he* knew he hadn't hit Puggy, and *I* knew he hadn't hit him, and he knew I knew and there wasn't a thing he could do about it!'

Then there was the old man who lived alone in a bare little house with a large and tidy garden. He had a passion for plastic garden gnomes, and must have had at least a hundred arranged in rows across his lawn. He must have picked each one up separately every week in order to mow the grass, and in winter they were all brought indoors and kept stored in a big cupboard.

Another poodle owner is not only a superb gardener but also makes the most gorgeous cream sponge I have ever tasted. At one time she always made it specially on trimming days so that I could have some with my coffee, and I once told her not to send flowers to my funeral but a cream sponge, and I would leave instructions that it

133

should be buried with me.

Another customer told me that one night her husband went up to bed early leaving her to lock up. She let the poodle out for her final duties while she went about the house shutting windows etc. She saw the dog shoot upstairs and assumed she had gone to her basket in their bedroom as usual, so proceeded to take a bath and don a clean night-dress before going to bed herself. But when she threw back the clothes on her bed in order to get in, what a sight – what a smell! Sheba had taken the opportunity while in the garden to roll herself in some choice attar of fox and had gone to ground between Mum's clean sheets!

Her mistress saw red. Cursing freely she hauled the luckless poodle out and into the bathroom, where she was obliged to bath her thoroughly, necessitating the long and tedious combing and drying process afterwards. Then the bedclothes must be removed, put in soak and replaced with clean dry ones, and last of all her owner needed another bath herself and yet another clean nightie. She was still furious when she went to bed, and her fury was not abated by what she saw on looking around for the offender. There she was, a little black face apprehensively showing the whites of her eyes from the shelter of her Dad's bed, tucked into his sheltering arm, while his voice crooned reassuringly, 'There, there, Daddy's little darling, never mind wicked Mummy, you're Daddy's little dog!'

Then there was the time when a sober business man came to my house and burst into tears because his dog was dead. He wanted my assurance that the poor little chap had gone to heaven. This was an embarrassing situation, especially as the dog had been one of the worst tempered animals I've ever had to handle, so that I couldn't help thinking that if he'd gone anywhere it might well have been to another place. So I told him I thought dogs deserved heaven every bit as much as humans, and this at least was true.

When I first began clipping poodles I shared the popular view that they were silly little creatures, all nerves and yap, mere walking tonsures. I don't think so now. True, there are such poodles, but it is usually the owners who are to blame, because more than any other breed I know, the poodle will become what it is made. I even know a case of a very immature poodle which changed homes at the age of seven on the death of her aged mistress, and on going to new owners who treated her as a normal dog altered completely to become what they expected. The astounding thing was that in her first home her coat was fine, thin and silky like that of a poodle puppy, but after a year of two with her new family, to my amazement she suddenly grew a tough springy adult coat, very dense and creamier in colour than her previous immature fluff. She is now fifteen and very active for her age. She is also clean in the house whereas her first mistress had never been able to house-train her – another puppy weakness, I suppose.

The average poodle is a lively, sensitive and affectionate companion and probably above the average level of intelligence among breeds. He can also have his quirks and fancies.

Pepe was another fifteen-year-old poodle who would eat nothing but fried lamb's liver. He was so fond of this that as soon as his mistress came in from the butcher's he would jump eagerly around her as she unpacked her basket. While she fried it he would sit drooling beside the cooker and could hardly wait for it to cool and be put down for him.

One day she thought she would economize. Lamb's liver was too expensive, twice the price of ox liver. She would buy the cheaper variety – he'd never know the difference.

Oh no? No Pepe came to meet her when she came in. In spite of her cheerful calls and inviting chirrupings of 'Dinner, boy,' he remained obstinately in his basket while the ritual frying took place. She cut it up and put it down, but she had to collect him bodily and place him nose to dish. He turned away in disgust.

'You eat it,' she said, and shut him into the kitchen while she went into the garden to hang out her washing. When she came back there was no sign of the liver. Or the plate. She found them pushed right to the back of the space between the wall and cooker, with the plate neatly overturned on top of the meat.

'You monkey, you will eat it,' she said, and this time shut him in the lounge with the offending meal while she went out for an hour. Once again the food disappeared complete with plate, and this time it took longer to trace. In fact she began to wonder whether he had somehow managed to swallow both.

Eventually she pulled the settee away from the wall. Nothing to be seen – or was there? Yes, a suspicious bump in the vinyl floor covering. Pepe had clawed it up and actually buried the hated meal, once again upside down, beneath it.

Pepe never did eat that ox liver. His owner gave in and made a second trip to the butcher's for some lamb's liver. He enjoyed that all right and the other went into the dustbin. So much for economy. But how did he know right from her first coming home that the liver wasn't what he usually had? He had always been very much a one-woman dog and for fifteen years had lived with all he had for his mistress. There can be no doubt that he was thoroughly tuned in to her mind. It was telepathy.

Although I learnt the art of trimming the hard way and have never been able to say 'I was trained' I have taught several others who therefore can! A local vet once sent his niece to me with the request that I train her. She was a young French Canadian girl over here on a visit, and she told me that her father had promised to buy her her own poodle parlour if she learnt to trim. But in Canada, she said, it was a closed shop and an outsider could not get tuition anywhere.

I was willing to help but was rather taken aback when she added that she was going home at the end of the week! This gave us six days, but in fact she only came for four, being ill one day and doing last-minute shopping the next. As I was already fully booked I could do nothing but let her come with me while I worked. I made her take copious notes and she asked a lot of questions, but when I offered to let her take the clippers over the back of a dog (the safest bit) she was too nervous to touch them. She said she would have to practise on her own poodles first.

Perhaps her time was not completely wasted because her questions were mainly concerned with how to tie the dogs up to make sure they couldn't bite. The idea that a properly handled dog would be relaxed and confident, wouldn't try to bite and therefore needed no tying was obviously a completely new revelation to her. She saw me do enough dogs to realise that it was true but still couldn't quite believe it when we parted.

On leaving she asked me for a certificate which she could hang in her parlour to prove she had been trained! This set me a poser as I wished to be both kind and truthful. I finally reconciled these aims as much as possible with a neatly written statement that she had received a short course of instruction and was ready to begin trimming. The ambiguities in this satisfied both of us. I hope she got her parlour and that my note, suitably framed, did grace its wall; she was a nice girl.

I charged her six pounds. I felt this was rather a lot for value received, but she had given me a good deal of extra work and one or two headaches. Poor lamb, she said earnestly that it seemed much too little as in Canada it would have cost her at least a hundred pounds, but we left it at six and parted good friends.

PART THREE
Breeding

Brand new puppies in a row
Only know one place to go –
Close to that Shape so like their own,
Smelling of nectar, warmth and home.

Puppies opening their eyes
View the world in slow surprise.
Such light! And with their gums they try
The taste of everything they eye.

Puppies learning how to lap
Don't want to feed, they'd rather nap.
Feet in the bowl he snorts and blows,
Then licks it off another's nose.

Puppies run on fat new feet,
Admire their toes and lose the beat,
Sit down, consider, then slowly creep
To join the pile of pups asleep.

Brand new teeth in puppies' jaws,
Everything he nips and gnaws.
Where'er he looks he pokes his nose,
And see how visibly he grows!

Puppies ready to be sold,
Not too young and not too old
May their owners see my care
And take them in, their hearts to share.

13
Brand new puppies

Trimming has provided the bulk of my income for a long time now. I get a mental and artistic pleasure from my job which prevents it palling and assures me daily that it is the right one for me. There is also another consideration which has weighed with me. When I began trimming as a serious career I needed, have always needed, and still need, a job which would enable me to keep my own dogs and go on breeding the occasional litter. Because to me that has always been the very nub of the dog keeping game.

When we were children Nell and I used to plan the kennels we were to have when we grew up. We were to breed Airedales and Great Danes, and spent a lot of time choosing the flowers and creepers we were to plant round the kennels to make them look beautiful.

It never happened like that, worse luck, and for poor Nell it never happened at all, but from that time on I always had the idea that I would become a breeder one day. There was no shall I, shan't I; I regarded it as not only desirable but inevitable. I belonged firmly with those who regard dog breeders as a race apart, the guardians of mysteries which cannot be learned from books, and I yearned to join their ranks. I thought – and I still think – that the person who produces a glorious pedigree dog enriches the earth as much as the one who grows beautiful flowers. And I wanted to be a good breeder.

Good breeders may have big kennels specializing in one, two or more breeds. They have kennel prefixes well known in the show ring and are jealous of their reputations. Or they may be private breeders with perhaps only a very small number of bitches kept as house pets. In either case a lot of planning, thought and intelligent care goes into the production of strong sound puppies of high quality. These breeders will want a lot of satisfying on such points as where a prospective purchaser lives, whether the garden is fenced and whether the puppy will have sufficient company. They are not selling a tin of beans and really care about each puppy's future prospects.

When I bought Jane, my cocker spaniel, I was thrilled to go into a new breed which I had long admired, and hoped very much that I would be able to show her, as this was something that I had never done. But most of all I saw her as my passport to an exciting new world of pedigrees and puppies.

First of all, however, I had to find a suitable sire. This seemed to be no problem as a friend had a very fine young dog which she was anxious to get mated. It seemed ideal to me in my inexperience, and both canine parties were all for the proposed union. But this part of the process is by no means as foolproof as one would think. My friend had also been reading up on the subject without apparently understanding it too well, for just as the lad, all enthusiasm, was about to effect his first stud, she suddenly grabbed him and pulled him off! This completely clobbered the project for that day. When I had sufficiently recovered my equanimity to enquire why she had done this, she explained that the books said the dog should be lifted off the bitch and turned for their mutual comfort. She had merely been a little – but disastrously – previous.

As it is possible for a bitch to become pregnant after a very brief contact indeed I did not feel that I could take her to another dog after this, so I had to wait a further six months for my first puppies.

I reported this fiasco to Jane's breeder, a simply splendid old lady who was sympathetic but informed me that it was probably just as well, as Jane's first husband had been a black and white, and although very well bred he was therefore not really suitable as a mate for her. Cockers with coloured patches on white are called particolours, reds and blacks are called solids, and never the twain should meet, as the result could easily be mismarked puppies which would have a materially reduced market value.

Mrs H. also gave me a great deal of very useful firsthand information and tips. One of these latter was the importance of keeping reliable records of seasons, matings, litters, and so on. She showed me hers – a dog-eared red notebook which she euphemistically referred to as 'my bunk-up book'. I don't keep a bunk-up book myself; details of seasons, matings, due dates, etc., all go into my diary, but because of her advice I do keep a breeding record with details of all puppies, the addresses of their owners and sometimes notes of their deaths.

As a result of my first experience with Jane I decided to have no more to do with privately owned dogs but to go to a top kennel and use a proved stud dog managed by an owner who knew the ropes. With the marriage arranged over the phone I then had a long and arduous journey to accomplish by public transport. To add to the hazards of the journey it was snowing. I mention this because one of the odder aspects of my early career as a dog breeder was the fact that for some years, whenever I took a bitch to be mated it always *was* snowing.

Anyway we arrived safely and Jane was duly mated to an extremely handsome black dog. I was rather disappointed that I didn't see the mating. Jane was whisked away to the kennel quarters for the ceremony while I was told to wait in the quite plushy reception room. I did think

143

this was rather taking advantage of my inexperience, as the owners should at least be invited to see the dog once the mating is in progress or she has no way of knowing whether the right dog has been used – or whether the bitch has in fact been mated at all. However there is no doubt that some pet owners can behave in quite an extraordinary way on these occasions, and a fit of the vapours on Mum's part can easily react on a nervous bitch to the point of making it impossible to get her to accept the dog.

In this case I have no doubt that Jane was in fact mated to the dog stated, who was brought out for me to see before I went home. My disappointment stemmed from the fact that I had not so far seen a mating and still had no firsthand experience in this important aspect of breeding and dog management to aid me in the future.

However you can imagine I was agog with excitement as the weeks went by and it became apparent that Jane was indeed pregnant. I fed her carefully, a necessary precaution as Jane was an exceedingly greedy dog whose appetite gave no guidance to her needs. I knew that proper feeding of the bitch at this time would not only safeguard her but lay the foundations of good strong constitutions for her puppies, and I was determined that those pups were going to have everything I could give them to assure perfection.

As regards the actual whelping I was determined not to miss a thing. But the best-laid plans . . . Jane came belting into the kitchen one day in her usual headlong manner and wolfed a plate of sausage-meat put down for the cat. She was very partial to this delicacy but it was not allowed her as it invariably disagreed with her. In the present situation you could say it was not so much sausage-meat as a red herring.

I took the ensuing disturbances to be the result of this self-indulgence, because Jane's puppies were not due for another week. After seeing her out into the garden a good many times I felt it was safe to go to bed. I have always tried to get my whelping box ready well in advance. This was just as well, because when I got up next morning there they were, four black and two gold puppies, dry, shining, and already full of milk. They certainly did not look premature, but although I checked dates and counted weeks over and over again, there was no doubt about it. In spite of the books' firmly asserted statements that puppies could not survive if born more than four days either early or late, there they were, seven full days early and quite clearly with every intention of surviving and enjoying it.

I rushed upstairs to tell the family the glad news, and returned to find her cleaning number seven, another gold. And that was all I saw of the birth of my long looked-forward-to first litter!

Although a week premature, these seven puppies were all strong and well formed, with shiny coats and a very good idea of how to deal with the milk bar. The books were certainly wrong here, because since then several other such cases have come to my notice. In each case it was the dam's first litter, and the bitches involved have included such varied breeds as miniature schnauzers, Old English sheepdogs, Yorkies and others. First litters do seem to have a tendency to come early.

So my first pups were really very little worry, especially as Jane was a naturally talented mother. I was probably luckier there than I realised, although when I chose the cocker as a breed I had noted that they were supposed to be good in this important respect.

Jane had been a little flighty before she had her puppies. Not exactly nervous, but if spoken to by a stranger she would dance about wildly, making excited squeaking and yelping noises, and no one outside the family could put a hand on her. It was wonderful to see with what a steady, sure instinct she set about the job of looking after her bonny babies, washing, feeding and comforting them. The only thing was that she was obviously not happy to hear me leave the house while she was nursing them. I would hear a shrill anxious yip as I closed the door, and she once startled my little girl considerably by flying at her when she came home from school and went unsuspecting into Jane's room while I was out.

I found this trust in me very touching. I still do, for all my bitches are the same. That fool Toffee took it so far as to insist on my sitting beside the whelping box and holding her paw between arrivals!

Jane's second litter was not so successful. Only four puppies this time, and one of these died at birth. They were the result of an April mating with a lovely dog who showed so little interest in her that she was once more whisked away to the kennels without me in the hope that he would be more active in his usual surroundings. This time I do have serious doubts as to whether he was in actual fact the father of the litter, but there was nothing I could do about it. I had to go down there twice, a grim journey as in spite of the date there was on both days a thick carpet of snow. A freak storm had taken the tops off all the birch trees right across southern England. Trains were erratic and buses not running. In spite of the fact that it was his dog's apathy that made my second trip necessary, the breeder charged me a high fee – and then owing to the international situation I practically had to give the puppies away.

However, I did at last witness and officiate at the birth of a litter, and a very absorbing experience I found it.

It was sheer over-keenness that made me not only stay up all night with her, but sleep in the same room for a week. It was lucky I did. On the second night she began to be sick, on a lavish scale. What she brought up was all water, and between bouts she drank still more.

Being a devoted mother she did all her vomiting right there in the box with her children. Fortunately I had plenty of newspaper laid in because without constant changing of their bedding the puppies would all have been drowned or died from exposure by morning. My efforts rewarded me with three live puppies, a pile of sodden newspaper a yard high, and a superstitious belief that I must sleep with my bitch and her new family for the first week. I still do, and have never lost a puppy during that period by its being overlaid or dying of chill in some corner of the room after managing to fall out of the cosy box.

I would advise all amateur breeders to do the same. Not like the owners of a small mongrel bitch who told a neighbour that they had shut her in a small cupboard to have

146

her unwanted puppies so that they could sleep undisturbed by her screams. Or the breeders of a planned litter who told me proudly that they had five beautiful puppies – their Alsatian had had ten and they had lost only five. Rather shaken by what was to me an unacceptably high mortality rate I asked them the cause of death.

They didn't know. Like the unhappy mongrel their bitch had been left alone all night to 'get on with it,' and in the morning the score was five dead and five doing well. Of course if owners like these had been in attendance I suppose the death rate might have been even higher.

Personally I think there is nothing quite like that tingle of excitement that comes when I detect the first almost invisible trembling of my expectant bitch. Then she begins to pant and fidget and I can tell anyone who wants to know, 'She's started!'

An exciting time it is, but oh, how it can try the patience. It's as well to be ready and well provided with all the necessities from glucose and torch to newspapers and wellies – not forgetting one's mundane everyday household shopping – for from the off you will be tied by invisible strings to your patient, possibly for a matter of several days. Torch and wellies? I wish I had a pound for every time I have patiently tracked my bitch round the dark rainy garden when she has decided that she really must go out, forcing me to walk behind, mac round my shoulders, pyjama trousers tucked into my boots, light trained on the relevant spot just in case she deposits a puppy in the long grass and runs in without noticing it – a long shot in a million I should think, but I can't help myself.

The vet who used to attend Jane told me that when it came to a whelping nothing would ever surprise her. I always remember that remark during that long irritating limbo known as The First Stages.

Jane got on with the job of producing her two families in a businesslike way and wasted little time on the job. It was Bamu who showed me what waiting in The First Stages could really be. With my scanty apprenticeship in cockers you can imagine how excited I was when Bamu was about to produce my first ever litter of Airedales. As I watched

147

her taking her ever more sedate exercise as the date approached she seemed to me like a trim and cuddly Earth goddess, symbol of fecundity.

Two days before her due date she went into The First Stages. I banished the family from the living-room, where her somewhat ramshackly litter box was situated in the snuggest recess, made myself a cosy bed on the settee and prepared for a siege. This went on for two days. Two days in which I hardly dared take my eyes off her! My persistence was at last rewarded by seeing the unmistakable ripple of a genuine labour pain pass down her back. At last The First Stages had become the second stages and now she should soon produce her first child.

But did she? No. After about ten minutes she was to all intents and purposes back again in The First Stages! I could easily have missed the signs that she was in fact past them if I hadn't been watching, so I suppose it paid off in the end. After an hour without result I sent for the vet who told me it was a case of uterine inertia. An injection of pituitrin started things going again and before long Bamu's first puppy had arrived. I was more than relieved, especially when several more followed in the next two hours. Things slowed down then but with six puppies in the box I felt I could at last give way to my long-fought desire for sleep. Next morning there were seven puppies in the box, just as with Jane. The newcomer was a little bitch, joining her one sister (Toffee) and five brothers in the nest. We called her Topsy because she had apparently 'just growed'.

Bamu suffered with uterine inertia with all her litters. I believe some breeds are more liable to it than others, and it seems to affect sensitive or highly-strung bitches the most. Bamu was very sensitive, but I think I was largely to blame because she was reacting to my over-anxiety and too much fussing. Remember that there was a very strong bond of love between us. It mattered desperately to me that she should be all right. She knew this and was responding by waiting for me to resolve the matter and get her out of this fix. In other words she expected me to produce these puppies without her having to exert herself, let alone go through pain to do so!

It took me years to learn this lesson, and even now I must always have my bitch within sight or sound during this period. It is a mistake to keep the bitch in during The First Stages. She will not want to leave home while she feels like that and it would be stupid to make her, but she can be encouraged to move around the house, or better still, the garden if the weather is good. It will make the waiting time seem shorter for both of you and she will be easier in both body and mind.

My bitches when in The First Stages spend a lot of time and effort digging large holes in the garden. I let them get on with this as I believe the exercise helps to bring the puppies down and make for an easier whelping. It is touching to see the seriousness with which they set about this task. They are always helped by the other canine members of the family, who are intensely interested and are content to show quite clearly that when it comes to digging a nursery it is the lady in waiting who is boss and they take their orders from her.

Topsy, the little girl who was the last born in Bamu's first litter, was very small and whined a lot, which worried both Bamu and me a great deal. If it happened today I would recognise the hunger-wail immediately. Topsy just wasn't getting enough milk.

I didn't realise at first what was wrong, but every now and then I made Bamu lie on the hearthrug and got Topsy out for a private tea, suckling from the more abundant nipples without competition from the lustier members of the bunch. This probably saved her life, and in the end she grew up as big and strong as Toffee.

When it came to Toffee's turn to have puppies I must admit I had my doubts, for unlike her very feminine mother Toffee was the very prototype of the 'doggy' bitch. However, I got her mated (it was June but we arrived in a flurry of snow) and in due course set up a brand new box, tailor-made to fit her Amazonian proportions, in the accustomed alcove in the sitting-room, and endeavoured to interest her in it. No use. Bamu scratched luxuriously in its deep newspaper, Silver the cat purred contentedly in its depths, but Toffee, after one casual glance, disregarded it with her typical thoroughness.

I didn't let it worry me. When she came into hard labour I shut the other two out of the room and waited. Toff hadn't a clue, and her main emotion when the pains first caught her seemed to be indignation. She decided she needed to go out into the garden. There was a narrow flower-bed in front of the french windows, and as she jumped over it her firstborn literally fell out into the soft wet earth all among the scarlet and gold dwarf dahlias.

The immediacy of Toffee's reaction drew first a gasp of amazement and then a feeling of admiration for this unique animal from me. She turned instantly, apparently in mid-air, seized the whelp, complete with mud overcoat and a few petals, and shot back into the hitherto totally ignored box, where she quickly gave him a thorough clean-up and then attended to herself. It was quite obvious that no one could tell *her* anything about having puppies. She then went on to produce six more, all born in the box. It is curious how many of my bitches have begun their reproductive careers with a litter of seven. I had no registered prefix in those days, but if I had known how often this number was to recur I might have chosen Heptomad, which means 'a set of seven'.

Toffee was a curiously efficient mother. Curiously, because after taking a long day's sleep among her infants to recover from the strain of producing them, she returned to her old roaming and running habits. Yet she always appeared at feeding times, stepping quietly into the box to nurse them and give them a ruthlessly thorough topping and tailing before getting out once more to check all the doors and fences in the hope of finding a weak spot. Yet her puppies were never dirty or whiny and grew rapidly and without check.

I have at present five bitches spanning four generations, and it is sweet to see the consideration shown to the pregnant bitch by her companions. She is no longer teased to join in their boisterous games. If she decides to dig an air raid shelter in the garden they will help her, but only if she wishes, and as her time draws near they will respect her wish for privacy.

When one of my bitches was scratching up the litter box in her First Stages, we had a visit from a fine young dog who always had a romp with the girls in the garden. This was going on when I heard a bloodcurdling snarl. Poor Timmy had tried to dash into the kitchen for a cooling drink but found his way firmly barred by the mother of the mum-to-be, who was definitely allowing NO outsiders into the house while her daughter was making ready to have a new family.

During the long gruelling business of whelping (gruelling for the human involved, anyway) the rest of the family wait quietly in another room, listening intently to every little noise and 'hoovering' me avidly whenever I go back to them.

If the bitch concerned needs to come through this room on her way to and from the garden, they will crowd round her sniffing and wagging their tails. She will not growl, but stand motionless with new dignity until they let her pass through. Having relieved herself she re-enters like a cannonball which none of the others is so foolish as to try to delay. She rushes back to her infants in the box and the job of producing the rest.

I tell the others that Stormy (or whoever it is) is having some little babies. They show much pleasure, probably at having what they already knew confirmed in words. Possibly they are relieved to know that this somewhat incompetent and slow-on-the-uptake head of the household is abreast of the facts.

The day after the birth they are all very eager to see the new arrivals, but cannot be allowed to enter the maternity ward in deference to the new mother's need for rest and quiet and no worries. They go into the garden to do sentry duty, and for the next two months will be somewhat noisier than usual until all the puppies are sold.

It will be all of a week before I can slip them in one at a time to see the new arrivals in Mum's absence. But surprisingly soon she will allow them to walk in and out of the room whether she is there or not. Touchingly, she has

151

complete faith in me and from the very first will tolerate uncomplainingly any human visitor as long as I am there too.

14

Puppies opening their eyes

Since the largest number of puppy deaths occur before the whelps are two weeks old it obviously makes good sense to take special care of them during this period.

It's a moot point whether the biggest factor in their well-being is their mother or just plain warmth. Certainly they can survive without her, but cold is a frequent killer. It so happens that I like my house hot – you could cook a cake in my sitting-room – so I can survive in the tropical atmosphere of my whelping room with little discomfort.

My habit of sleeping there for the first week keeps me up to the mark too. A room which is unbearably hot to work in can get surprisingly chilly when you are lying down covered with a single blanket. Imagine how much chillier yet it must feel if you weigh less than a pound, are protected by the thinnest layer of fine hair and are struggling for survival in a new element. So I keep the heat around eighty for the first week; after all, a dog's normal temperature is a hundred and one and the puppies are lying in the coolest place, near the floor. You'd think the bitch would object, but she doesn't, she seems very content to doze blissfully with her lovely new family during this time.

You can of course use an infra-red lamp, and most breeders do, but knowing my bitches I think they would find this disturbing – and since I read of a basin of water left under a lamp being found frozen next morning my faith is a little shaken. So I shall probably go on using the old Turkish bath trick; after all, it has served me well up to now.

If there is a fairly low cover over the nest, for instance if the litter has been born in something like a tea-chest, they will probably be kept warm enough by the heat generated by their mother. However, this is not often convenient with a large breed, and personally I like to have a clear view of what is happening in that box.

When I felt sufficiently sure of my destiny to have a proper whelping box made I ran a tape down and across Toffee when she was lying asleep flat on her side. I felt that any box big enough to hold my monster in that position was likely to be big enough to cover all future requirements.

I took a lot of trouble designing it because it had to be capable of being taken to pieces and packed flat when not in use. By sheer luck I hit on a design which was perfect. Not only could the front be used folded down or fastened up according to the age and agility of its inmates, but it could be taken out altogether to enable them to run in and out as they got more active. It could then be placed on top, •not only converting the box into a draughtproof indoor kennel, but also providing a convenient broad shelf for storing the piles of clean newspaper for which there never otherwise seems to be enough room.

Airedales often have big litters running into double figures. It used to be a common practice to cull the weaker puppies – in fact I believe that in Germany no one is allowed to rear more than six puppies in a litter. Thank goodness we don't have to do that here, because with modern foods and methods there is absolutely no reason why every viable puppy should not be kept to grow into as good a dog as any other.

On one occasion Sunny's daughter Sadie produced five enormous offspring only four days after her mother had had a litter of twelve, of which eleven had lived. Sadie had more milk than her babies needed. Sunny on the other hand had hardly any. Apparently Sadie herself felt that there was an obvious answer to this problem, for the next day I found her crying outside Sunny's door.

I took her back to her own room, then quietly abstracted the three smallest babies from Sunny's box. I put them into the 'cradle', a tomato skip which I often put puppies into while cleaning the box, and took them to Sadie. She was feeding her own family and opened one eye when she saw the cradle. I lifted it into a vacant corner of her box and she sat up to sniff its contents, then lay down again quietly. I gently put the three tiny puppies into the box and watched.

The three started straight away towards the source of warmth and the scent of milk. I could see that Sadie was watching, but she made no move and permitted them to nuzzle in among her own mighty brood. They looked very comical, like three mice among a row of hippopotami although they were four days the elder, but they were strong enough and soon were feeding gratefully from this literally overflowing fountain of life.

I had been bottle-feeding these puppies – in fact they would not otherwise have still been alive – but once they got to Sadie's land of milk and honey they had no further use for the bottle! They had all weighed less than seven ounces as against Sadie's which had all weighed in at birth at a pound and a quarter, but they soon made up for it and by the time they were sold they were as big as their foster-brothers.

Another thing I have been told is that any healthy Airedale bitch should be able to feed ten puppies unaided. Maybe, but why should she? And why should those mites be engaged in so grim a struggle for survival? It never seems to me that whelps – that is, puppies before their eyes are open – are babies at all. They are simply very small creatures fighting for their lives, and that is never a sentimental matter. At two weeks they should be safely established in this world, more warmly protected by their growing coats and insured against minor disasters by a growing layer of fat. They can then afford the luxury of babyhood, and with misty eyes open and newly chubby shapes they begin to look the part.

Small puppies at a crowded milk bar get pushed out by bigger and stronger ones. It is because they go hungry that they become smaller still in comparison with the others as they get weaker. They may even die. So if I see this happening I get out my feeding bottles and begin topping up: and what a difference that first artificial feed makes! I've found too that it pays to top up *all* the puppies – Butch, who appears to be twice the size of Tich may be ravenous because he just can't get enough to fill his big tummy. If he knocks back an ounce of milk mixture it means that more will be available from their mother for his weaker brothers and sisters.

Twelve ounces is a good average weight for an Airedale at birth, but I have successfully reared tinies half that weight which have grown to full size, been healthy, handsome and happy, and lived to a ripe old age.

Puppies in the nest are the biggest timewasters known to woman. I – and a lot of other people – have sat by our dogs' boxes by the hour, completely hypnotised by the Lilliputian gruntings and squirmings of these incredible little beings.

When they are a few days old there comes the vexed question of docking and dew-clawing. Jane's breeder insisted on coming to do Jane's first litter for me because she didn't trust any mere vet to cut the tails to the right length, and countless valuable puppies have certainly been spoilt like this. I partly dreaded this and partly looked forward to it, for I was still eager to learn at first hand all I could about dogs. Besides, I felt that if I submitted my puppies, who hadn't any say in the matter, to this operation, then I should at least have to guts to stay and assist.

So I did, and she kindly explained to me what she was

156

doing and why, although I had at that time not the slightest intention of ever doing the job myself. However, when Jane's second litter arrived Mrs H. was unable to come until they were ten days old. She said this would still be all right because docking can legally be done at any time before the puppies' eyes open, but I felt it was leaving it too late.

Faced with this contretemps I asked myself – could I do it? Armed with the reflection that there were only three puppies, and feeling decidedly shaky, I nerved myself to do the job. Had it been a large litter I don't think I could have faced it. But I forced myself because I knew it had to be done and done soon. After the first puppy it didn't seem so bad, and I successfully completed the job and have docked all my puppies since, with the exception of Chai's seven. In her case I felt her mental state to be so abnormal that it would be wiser to devote all my energies to managing her and leave the actual job to the vet.

Docking of course is a fashion regarded by many as a relic from more barbaric times. However, in some cases there are good reasons for it. Undocked working spaniels can slash their tails to ribbons and lose a good deal of blood owing to their habit of threshing them excitedly when working among the brambles. Terriers are supposed to have been docked to lessen the chances of being grabbed by a fox or badger when retreating head first from an earth, while with heavy coated dogs such as poodles and Old English sheepdogs it is a very hygienic practice.

Old English in particular often get absolutely disgustingly filthy at the rear end even now. A friend of mine who ran a poodle parlour told me that they once weighed the mass of dried and and matted faeces which they had removed from the back end of one of this breed and found that it weighed more than twenty pounds! Of course the skin underneath this sort of muck, which has possibly taken months to accumulate, is usually indescribably raw and inflamed.

Imagine the predicament of such a dog if it also carried a heavy bushy tail across this region. Many would certainly be infested with maggots and I am sure some would even die. So I do think that in such breeds docking is not cruelty but the most genuine kindness.

This also applies to the removal of dew-claws, the 'thumbs' which dogs have an inch or so above the fore-feet. These often cause a lot of trouble as they can catch in things like wire and tear right up the leg. Personally I think all dogs should have them removed, although it is the fashion in some breeds to retain them. In some, such as the Pyrenean Mountain Dog, it is also considered a good show point to have them on the back legs too, and sometimes they are double. But where the breed custom calls for their removal or leaves it optional I would always remove them, and I think most vets would agree with me. You may say that nature designed dogs with dew-claws, but she didn't design their modern habitat, with lurking traps of hidden wires, glass, etc., to catch them as they race over the ground.

As to docking, although we would no doubt soon get used to seeing long-tailed boxers, corgis and terriers and might even come to prefer them, I am against a sudden ban on docking on humane grounds. This sounds contra-dictory, but the fact is that many breeds are at present bedevilled with various problems caused by hereditary diseases, nervous and temperamental difficulties and bad movement. Most breeders are making honest and praise-worthy efforts to solve these problems, but what would happen if docking were suddenly prohibited? They would be forced to set about breeding a suitable tail, and these more important issues would be bound to suffer. Many otherwise undesirable dogs would be bred from, while others much better but with 'wrong' tails would be ignored.

Perhaps it would be an acceptable compromise if breed-ers were given a twenty year deadline. If they knew that docking was definitely going to be banned at the end of that time they might well make great strides towards get-ting their ideal tails by then without damage to their breeds.

On the face of it it seems a dreadful thing to chop off the end of a puppy's tail, but it should not be forgotten that at a few days old the tail is no more than a stiffish jelly, and if the operation is done properly there will be no blood, no upset to the bitch, and so little pain that it is expressed in a surprised squeak and forgotten as soon as she goes back and feeds them.

My Westie Peggy had a nasty trick of nipping her puppies when they got on her nerves, and when she did, how they would scream. The little yip of a puppy at docking is nothing to it, so if docking is cruel then to be logical I should have taken Peg away from her little sons, who although undocked, were obviously suffering a lot more.

Puppies seem very imperfectly developed prior to the opening of the eyes, and when they do open them it is not all at once, like the enchanted princess on the kiss of the prince. No, one simply sees one morning a little gleam of reflected light in the corners of some of those tight-shut peepers, often so small that you aren't quite sure you're not imagining it, and often only in one eye, not both! But by the next morning all the puppies will probably have prised up both eyelids even if the eye still looks a bit narrow, and suddenly your squirming sausages have been transformed into little dogs.

No doubt the eyes are not able to bear the light until this event, but it is not always realised that the ears are also sealed and the whelps deaf. Certainly they know when their mother returns to them, possibly by scent, probably also by touch, feeling her vibrations through the floor of the box.

But do whelps have no intelligence up to this point apart from the instincts which help them find the source of food and teach them how to obtain it? I've read that the intelligence of a new-born puppy is like an electric circuit with the current turned off until the switch is thrown at three weeks of age. I wonder.

Jane had two dog puppies in her second litter which I named Buster and Squeaker. When they were only two days old Buster, seeking a more plentiful tap, crawled right across the nose of Squeaker, who was well plugged in and feeding heartily. I saw this because it happened while I was indulging in a spot of hypnotised puppy-watching.

To my surprise Squeaker promptly growled with a noise like a minute kettledrum, tiny but fierce. It amused me very much at the time, but strange to say, although they both grew up as sweet tempered as their mother they always knew and fought each other on the instant if by chance they met! Was it that accidental brush on their second day that started this lifelong antipathy?

More recently, I held up a blind Airedale whelp to show a friend. Squirming in my hands the puppy by chance closed her little mouth on the top of my finger. The usual reaction here would be for the whelp to begin sucking, but this one was already full up and content. Instead she gripped harder on my finger and attempted to shake it!

There was nothing aggressive in this reaction. By her movements, not only of her head but her whole body, it was plain to my friend and myself that at the age of ten days, and with her eyes still closed, Iris was playing!

15
Puppies learning how to lap

Bottle-feeding a large litter is a maddeningly lengthy process, especially if you have to clean their rear ends as well because the bitch is too dainty to demean herself with anything so coarse. I've tried repeatedly, but it really isn't possible to cope with more than one pup at a time.

First you must pick up a puppy, get it to spend a penny by tickling with damp cotton wool, then persuade it to feed from the bottle until full up, then put it aside in a large cardboard carton. Repeat until the whole litter has been transferred from the nest to the carton, then do the whole job again in reverse. True, the puppies will spend less time feeding on the return journey, but this is offset by the need to make them empty their bowels. You do this by rubbing around the anus with a pad of damp cotton-wool in imitation of the action of the bitch's tonge, and it is essential because without the stimulus of either of these methods the very young puppy is actually unable to evacuate, and that is very definitely not at all good for him.

Sunny's granddaughter Storm, who is a very big bitch, possibly as big as Toffee, could in her younger days feed a litter of ten or twelve completely unaided for as long as four weeks, but I've found this exceptional. When Sunny had her last litter after a very trying pregnancy she was so exhausted that she had only enough milk for two or three puppies – and there were eleven! In that case I treated them as a hand-reared litter and regarded anything they got from their mother as an extra. They all thrived, but oh, how I longed for the day when they would all be lapping from bowls.

Puppies that go for four weeks completely on the dam are easy to wean, but bottle-fed puppies can drive you out of your mind with their pernickety refusal to lap. As with the bottle, it is always the big strapping ones that are the most awkward. I've had to resort to starvation more than once to induce such a cussed customer to be more co-operative. Toots, a big pup who saw no reason to put his little snout into a bowl when he'd got me to make a bottle for him, was put to the bowl with every single one of his ten brothers and sisters separately before he finally gave in and found to his joy that eating this way was actually quicker and more fun.

I have two tricks which do help to reduce the agony (to me) of this stage. At the tender age of two weeks puppies may be given raw beef. Incredible but true, and once they've got the taste of it they love it. I buy best quality minced beef which can be mashed with warm water or put through the liquidiser if you have one. Not only does a quite minute quantity of beef, say half a teaspoonful, keep a puppy contented for far longer than before, but owing to their partiality for it they will readily learn to lap it much quicker than they will milk. By three weeks lapping is pretty well established as one of their accomplishments and they can usually be persuaded, even with a little argument, to use it for milk too.

All this of course has to be started on a one-at-a-time basis and is probably the cause of most breeders taking to drink. If this sounds too harsh, just remember that she has probably kicked off with an all-night (possibly two all-nights) whelping with considerable loss of sleep, and has been at full stretch both physically and emotionally ever since. She has all her other usual work still to do, and I personally have spent as much as *eight hours* in a single day feeding reluctant puppies. When I speak of resorting to starvation it has been a case of it's me or the pup. I've been at the far end of my tether and literally unable to go on. And of course, as in the case of Toots, the pup has been quite well able to cope with feeding but refusing with an obstinacy which has augured well for its future strength of character!

This is when my second trick comes in useful. It is just to obtain a shallow cardboard box from the greengrocer – the sort of thing that Dutch lettuces come packed in – and use it as a feeding tray. With a long shallow trough at one end – the ice cube tray from the fridge is a useful size and shape – you can put as many as three puppies in to feed together. When they start the scandalised back-pedalling at the sight of mass food which is one of their most irritating habits at this stage they can't go far nor fall off the table. If the phone rings you can put the whole lot on the floor and safely leave them for a few minutes, and when the resolute I-want-it-from-my-mum brigade persist in seeking their grub from the ceiling instead of the floor it is much easier to place a firm but kindly finger on their small snouts and guide them downwards. And any pup who sees the light and starts to lap is likely to indoctrinate any buddy who is at the trough with him. I find this a great nerve tonic at this time.

I like to know all my puppies individually and it is a help if each has a name. Choosing them is fun, as 'nest names' are not meant to be permanent and give me a chance to indulge in some really whacky ones. Usually they are descriptive. Characters described may be size – e.g. Buster, Bunter, Tiny, Tiddler or Mouse, but most often these names refer to white marks on the puppies. Airedales are born mostly black with tan noses and paws, but quite often they carry white patches on their chest or feet. The tan spreads extensively as they grow and these marks become much smaller. On the feet they will almost entirely disappear, but at three weeks they show up clearly and have been the inspiration for many nest names.

Spot, Dot, Stripe, Splash, Lefty, Twinkletoes – even Vesta, so called from her very conspicuous white vest – were all descriptive of white marks, and these puppies can then be identified by others who may be helping me with my litter as well as myself.

One of Storm's families, born in a very late cold spring, were all given flower names to the great amusement of everyone who heard them – Tulip, Daffodil, Crocus, Iris, Primrose, Snowdrop – even Aubretia, decorously shortened to Aubrey. Storm's own nest name was Lulubelle. A bit involved, that one. Her mother was Sadie, who is often called Lulu – a sort of endearment arising from Sadie Lou or Sadie Lulu. Storm (with whom I fell desperately in love when she was only two days old) was to me the most glorious and beautiful of all Sadie's daughters, hence Lulubelle. Well it makes sense of a sort to me if to no one else!

My children and neighbours' children are also freely allowed to name puppies at this stage. A ten year old at present studying this fascinating subject when not at school asked that one of my last litter be named Little Feet. He was. Why not? It doesn't matter – or does it? For the astonishing thing to me is how often their new owners decide to keep these names!

When Stephen was a little boy he invented the name Serrapin for one of Jane's daughters, and to my dismay she was Serrapin for months because her owners couldn't think of another. Eventually I persuaded them to shorten it to Sarah. Ophelia was renamed Dixie, but Hamlet was stuck with it and so was Vesta. Jumbo I am rather proud of, a really nice name for a big friendly dog . . . but – Sootfoot? At least it's a change from Susie.

All of my spring flower litter were renamed. Curiously enough the two bitches, Iris and Primrose, although going to quite independent owners in different districts, were christened Solar and Sula.

The real value of nest names is that they help me to keep track of individual puppies. To be sure that the puppy slow to feed is not always the same one. To check

164

that the little one who yelled so when he caught his foot is not limping afterwards. And to be able to predict that the middle-sized pup will probably end up a big one because he used to be the smallest member and is now rapidly catching up.

Rounder, fatter, more delectable day by day, and growing so fast that you can see the difference between night and morning, morning and evening. Now is the time when my puppies become so irresistible with that touching beauty peculiar to all healthy baby creatures.

Between three and four weeks of age I introduce into their diet minute quantities of all the different foods they will be reared on. They are still only playing at eating, but practice makes perfect, and by the time they are five weeks old they will be virtually independent of their mother. I can begin to cut down on her food and relieve her of the burden of feeding them altogether.

It always fascinates me to watch my bitch with her family, it is so miraculous to see how a sensible bitch knows instinctively what's best for her young. When constant nourishment is essential she will sleep day and night flat on her side while they feed and grow, but later she becomes more restless and sits up to do the job, obliging the puppies to make more effort to get at her. Later still she will stand up to feed them. If she's a bit previous at this stage some of the smallest members will need a little propping up at the bar. Nevertheless, with their size so greatly increased by then a large litter would hardly be able to feed all together unless she made room for them in this way.

Besides, their sharp baby teeth are through by now and they have no compunction about using them on her. This makes her hop and pull away from them and this is the first natural step towards weaning.

An intermediate step here is for the bitch to regurgitate her own partly digested food for her litter, and this is how wild dogs and similar species provide for their growing families. It is very rare for any of my bitches to do this, however, probably because my liberal early weaning system relieves them of the necessity; although an extra-maternal bitch may do so.

I am happy to say that with the exception of Chai all my bitches have been sensible and maternal in varying degrees. I remember that when Bamu was having trouble with uterine inertia with her first litter my vet, apologising for not staying with us as she had another whelping to attend, said she felt the other dog and owner needed her assistance more than we did.

When she came back she said it was a good job she had gone. On her arrival she found the owner crying in one armchair and the poodle shrieking in another. On picking it up she found that it had already borne a puppy, although both dog and owner were unaware of the fact as both were quite hysterical. As my vet was not one who suffered fools gladly I imagine she dealt pretty crisply with both of them. Tyro as I was I felt quite proud that she had considered me fit to leave!

When teaching my puppies to lap, I must first take each one on to a towel on my knee with a little deep bowl and do my best to get the message across, but it is a long and messy business and I usually transfer them to the shallow tray on the second day. Then I can breathe a sigh of relief for it means the worst is over. Reluctant feeders can share bowls with more advanced students and before long the whole bunch will be feeding enthusiastically from a row of dishes on the floor of their pen. True they will stand in it and spill a good deal, but no matter, they will lick each other clean with great enjoyment.

Many people believe in giving each puppy a separate bowl. I don't because I find that feeding all together from a long line of dishes placed end to end to form a trough makes the puppies eat greedily and that is what I want at this stage. There's no danger of the smaller ones going short, because there's plenty of room and always slightly more food than the combined gang can eat.

Soon a group of little footballs on legs staggers drunkenly away to sleep it off. Dinner time is over and it has occupied perhaps all of two minutes!

16
Puppies run . . .

When I tell people that I have 'x' number of puppies they tend to throw up their hands in horror. Obviously they are remembering the trouble they've had with just one puppy and are mentally multiplying it. Of course, for the one-off breeder it can be like that!

Owning a large and growing litter is never going to be a soft option, but forethought and organisation can make all the difference between strenuous fun and sheer hell. When my litter box is converted into an indoor kennel and the pups begin to run about, they immediately present another problem only too easy to imagine. However I have cunningly provided for this before they were even born by the erection of an indoor run, six feet square, made of light, rigid wire netting panels complete with gate. I cover the carpet with a square of really tough polythene, then put up the pen and erect the box in one corner.

In the bottom of the box I jam a roughly fitting layer of

thick cardboard and then cover this too with a pad of newspaper and all is ready. My bitches, when they come into labour, immediately rip up all the paper in the box and scrape a hole in the centre in an endeavour to get through the boards, through the floor and into the foundations. This is where the cardboard comes in, to prevent the puppies being born on the cold hard wooden box floor, because the bitch will not be able to scratch her way through it. All this except the cardboard will need changing afterwards, and then I make a new bed of shredded newspaper. This sounds like a long job but in fact is easily done while I am admiring the new family. It is easily taken out when soiled, is economical of newspaper and almost wipes out the danger of puppies getting trapped in a fold of the bedding and being overlaid or suffocated.

So when the front comes out of the box the babies are already provided with a safe playground, and the rest of the house is protected from dirt and damage. A big improvement on the time when bad weather forced us to give up our sitting-room to one of Bamu's litters! They had the french windows as their exit to the garden and I kept observation through the kitchen hatch. The family were remarkably good about it all but in spite of our removing all the furniture and rugs from the room beforehand it still had to be redecorated afterwards as twelve dirty little front paws had printed a very busy dado right round the bottom of the walls.

The new roof of the box is piled high with clean newspapers begged from friends, relatives and customers. I can literally never have too much. The combined box and pen now cover an area six foot square, and in spite of the thick plastic baseplate it needs paving with at least three layers of newspapers – whole newspapers, not sheets.

I've thought a lot about newspapers since I've been breeding dogs. First of all let me express the sorrow which all breeders must feel for the demise of so many *big* papers, and the regrettable trend towards the tabloid form. My luckiest haul was when I visited a house to trim a dog and the husband kept walking through the kitchen carrying piles of the *Financial Times* in mint condition.

168

When I diffidently suggested that if all this precious material was actually unwanted I could find a use for it, he practically clasped me to his bosom. Apparently he was a stockbroker who had gradually filled his study with it until he couldn't get in there himself. When I drove away my minivan was chock full. I couldn't see out of the rear windows and there was even a pile on the passenger seat. Unluckily these people were minding the dog for an absent relative, so I only went there the once.

My most maddening haul was an immense pile of large newspapers from an elderly couple who were my neighbours. The pile looked great, but when I came to use it I found that every double sheet had been separately folded four times! Apparently that was how they read it, taking a sheet each, changing over and then folding it up when they'd finished with it! Imagine the frustration and waste of time trying to spread them all out again to use in bulk. I had to use them because I was very short of paper at that time.

There are several Laws of Nature which come into play when you use papers for puppies. One is that they will immediately soil a clean sheet, and another is that they will never deposit their little offerings in the middle of a sheet but with great skill position them to soil the edges of as many as possible. Another is that no matter how carefully you pick up you will always get some of this goo on your fingers. As I said, these are Laws of Nature. It's no good fighting them and swearing is equally useless.

When I began tearing my papers into strips for bedding I learnt a new fact about newsprint – there is a grain in it and you can't tear straight if you try to tear against it. Tabloids need to be opened – and you'll never find the middle first time, another L. of N. – torn down the fold and then stripped across the page, but broadsheets go the other way. They too need to be torn down the middle, but each half must then be treated as a complete tabloid.

I've also learnt to keep my glasses with me when I'm changing the bedding, it's so maddening not to be able to read the story under a promising heading, and as is well known, old newspapers are always more interesting than today's.

I keep a plastic sack by the pen to take the soiled bedding, and when a litter is in full production they can fill it twice a day. Disposal of such quantities presents problems too. It's not as easy as you'd think to burn it. Don't forget it's both damp and comes in thick wodges, and even if you may have a bonfire and it's not raining, it won't burn well without a good deal of stirring. You certainly can't burn it in the kitchen boiler. Once I tried to compost it. I had that particular heap at the bottom of my garden for several years before it eventually rotted away.

In spite of all these drawbacks, however, newspaper has one cardinal virtue which outweighs them all. It is the only raw material which the breeder is going to need in bulk which comes free.

Puppies are surprisingly mobile right from birth, but it is not till their eyes open and they begin to focus on each other that they start to get right up on their legs and stagger about. I think this must be because of the ratio of weight to muscle, because I shall never forget how astounded I was when Toffee produced her strange little 'frog' puppy in her last litter. This tiny chap was nothing but skin and bone at birth, but so strong and determined that he immediately came right up on his feet and *walked* to the nearest nipple, where he proceeded to tank up without delay. He did not walk again till the usual time, but this incident shows that the instinct and machinery are all there right from the start.

It is very funny to see a small puppy trying to pull his brother's tail. By the time he has got himself together and made his grab either the tail has moved somewhere else or the would-be attacker has fallen over. Then he goes into a huddle with himself where you feel he is earnestly examining his failure and trying to find out what went wrong – always assuming that by now he hasn't forgotten what he wanted in the first place!

I believe in giving puppies plenty of scope. The indoor pen serves them well till they are about five weeks old, but then comes their first big change. They go out into the big outside kennel.

I'm lucky in having a large shed with room for a good-sized run behind it. Half the shed has been made into a puppy run with two wooden kennels inside it. I put a loose wooden floor down in this inside pen and cover it with deep sawdust. The small kennel which is going to be the puppies' bedroom is furnished with an enormous cushion made out of old curtains or such and stuffed with wood shavings.

I don't shut the pups into the small kennel at night; instead I hang a sack over the door to keep the warmth in, and no litter so far has failed to recognise that this is a good place to sleep. In fact I've found a neighbour's child curled up fast asleep on the big cushion before now!

After the first day in their new quarters I leave the inner pen gate open, also the door of the shed, and very soon the pups will be adventuring and exploring to the furthest corners of their new territory. They find plenty to amuse them. They get even hungrier and quickly become ever more active, strong and agile.

Giving free access to a grassy area has another advantage in that the puppies accept this as a good place to be clean in and when they go to their new homes they will be much easier to house-train than puppies which have always been indoors and therefore think that's the right place to go.

A sawdust run is much easier to manage than newspaper. Unfortunately it is not suitable for use indoors and also gets into the puppies' coats, looking rather grubby and causing them to scratch. And if there's one job I hate it's going with my sacks to the sawmill and begging abjectly for sawdust. Begging although I will have to pay for it and probably tip the man as well, and think myself lucky if I don't personally have to shovel it up into the bargain.

My bitches never move into the shed with their puppies although they will be anxious to visit them at meal times to see they are all right, and will stand willingly to let them feed. The other bitches will go up to see them too, partly to make sure no delicious fragment of puppy food is being sinfully wasted.

There is a great danger at this stage that the puppies

may develop kennel nerves through being too much alone and away from human contact. To combat it I encourage visitors and especially neighbouring children whom I can trust. I also, from the age of six weeks and onward, open the gate of the grass run and let the pups find their own way out and into the garden.

They enjoy this enormously. I never carry them forcibly out of their fenced run, but one by one they will emerge, and before long joyous pitched battles are going on in the bordering hedgerow for possession of the bumps and burrows constructed by their seniors. The long path down to the house is a bigger challenge, but soon the whole litter will be charging all over the garden, only scooting for cover when the big dogs set up an alarm of barking.

When Sunny and Sadie had their two families I ran all sixteen together as one litter in their outdoor quarters. There was no risk of getting them mixed up as Sadie's five were always easy to distinguish.

I find it a quite horrid sensation to have young puppies clawing at my legs when I go to feed them, and in this case tried to minimise it by creeping quietly into the kennel in an attempt to get the feeding bowls down and filled before they were properly awake. I could then make my getaway while they were still busy at the trough.

I didn't realise it, but this was a serious mistake. One day as I appeared in the doorway a puppy screamed in terror. With so many there I couldn't decide which one it was and thought no more about it at the time.

A week or two later, when over half the puppies had been sold, the remainder were, as I thought, all playing in the garden when I had occasion to go up to the kennel to fetch something. Again as I entered the doorway a puppy screamed. Spangles, one of Sunny's daughters which I had picked out for myself, had gone back to the kennel to rest and had been dozing in the inside run. My silent approach had struck terror into her poor little heart and she shot into the inner kennel. I had to follow her and haul her out bodily, paralytic with fright. I sat and nursed and comforted her for some time, carried her out into the bright sunlight and down to the house, offered her titbits

172

and kisses. She recovered for that time, but alas, for me she was ruined.

Although I kept her for nearly a year, and although she was fond of me, Spangles never completely got over her fear. When I want my dogs in from the garden I simply open the back door and call 'Everybody in!' and they all shoot straight inside. Not Spangles. She would stop dead as she reached the doorway. To get her in at all I had to stand out of sight and hope she would pass through before she caught sight of me, otherwise she would whip outside again before I could shut the door behind her.

I tried to overcome this by fussing and fondling her and she was pathetically anxious to receive this assurance of my affection, but in would barge the rest of the gang, and as soon as I tried to push them away Spangles would take fright and bolt. As I like my dogs extrovert and pushy all this irritated me very much and although I tried not to show it she wasn't fooled. The more annoyed I felt, the jumpier she got. The jumpier she got, the more I was annoyed. It was a vicious circle.

Luckily I suddenly had an enquiry not for a puppy but for a young bitch. A very nice family came to see her and to my surprise and relief she climbed up on to the father's lap, licked his hair and nibbled his ears, a compliment she had never paid to me. She went on approval, but they were delighted with her and sent me a beautiful photograph of her the next Christmas to prove it.

It was the right thing for her, but now I make sure my puppies hear me coming with their food before I loom up in that doorway, black and huge against the light.

My bitches are always good with their puppies when they are running around although I sometimes think they are sorely tried. Even my old cat Puddy insisted on fraternising with Bamu's and Toffee's puppies when they were placed in a pen in the garden. He would drop gracefully down in their midst, and rolling contemptuously on to his back, would proceed to take a refreshing dust bath in the middle of a circle of wondering puppies. They would dab at him wistfully with inquisitive black noses and fat paws that never quite dared to make actual contact. Having asserted his superiority and untouchability in this way, Pud would then quit the pen and stalk haughtily away.

As the puppies develop the mother gets a good deal of fun out of playing with them. The only thing wrong with Toffee as a mother was her habit of picking her children up by the back legs and swinging them round her head when they were at this stage. Airedale puppies grow very quickly and soon cease to be mere cuddly bundles of babyhood; still, that was no excuse for Toff. She loved playing with her children, it was just typical of her contrary genius that she should invent a game that always had to be stopped as soon as it started!

A more normal bitch plays games that are educational as well as enjoyable. She knocks her offspring about and often closes her great jaws about them but does not hurt them. She is showing them how to look after themselves in a rough-house, and every day they become stronger and more agile.

The other bitches also take an interest in the little ones and help to look after them. Solo's daughter Socks, who never had any puppies of her own, was particularly good with them although growling and snarling in a quite terrifying way most of the time. She had a way of standing rigid, while showing her impressive armoury of teeth at the offending babe. But baby was never impressed. He would stand up and put his paws on Socks' nose and try to pull out those same great beautiful white fangs with his sharp little milk teeth. If no one came to her rescue Socks would decide that she'd better humour him, push him down with a careful paw and begin washing his ears. He would like this and settle down to enjoy it.

All my bitches will suffer a good deal, even if not gladly, until Baby goes too far. Then there is a sudden snap and a snarl and Baby is getting out of it hell for leather, and will sit looking offended and be good for some time. The interesting thing is that he is never actually hurt by these small explosions even though his squeals may be deafening. I have come to think of these nips as the equivalent of the Cockney Grandma's 'good clip round the ear 'ole'. They certainly chasten the young delinquents as nothing I can do will.

It appears that puppies are born without any instinctive knowledge of the meaning of growling by others, and this is all part of their education which will help them when they come to approach strange dogs in later life.

Sometimes in summer one of the pups will be missing at bedtime. At such times I would call Socks and begin a tour of my big garden saying anxiously to her 'Where's that baby Socks?' She would take this seriously and was invariably the first to find the puppy, usually asleep underneath a shed or in a dusky hollow near the fence. She would remain on point while giving regular anxious barks until I went over and recovered the truant. Dear old Socks reminded me of the elephant 'Aunties' who run the herd crèches.

17
Brand new teeth

There are a lot of things to attend to before a litter can be sold. First they must be dosed for roundworm, and mine are done at three weeks and every fortnight thereafter until they go.

Kennel Club registrations are another duty and a constant headache. Because of the long time they take to come through they are unlikely to be completed by the date of sale, and because they are now so expensive it is like having a tooth pulled to send off the cheque before any money starts coming in from the puppies themselves. A big litter will cost fifty pounds or more to register, and fifty pounds will buy an awful lot of puppy food. Even if a good part of the litter is booked beforehand, you still have all your expenses to meet before any money comes in – and you must get your priorities right.

I took my kennel prefix, which is a kind of registered trademark, from the name of the house we had at the time – Caterways. Then each puppy has an individual name added. Breeders often name their litters alphabetically – all the puppies in the first litter will have registered names beginning with A, the next with B and so on. You see some interesting efforts towards the end of the alphabet!

In my earlier days I thought I would be clever and take my names from Shakespeare's plays. Thus I had a Hamlet litter, a King Lear litter and so on. I got some wonderful names from this source. Some that come to mind were Thunderstone, Great Axe, Joyful Trouble and Kettledrum. But unfortunately it became harder and harder to find them and I had to face the fact that the Bard didn't really put his back into the job of inventing names for dogs. I would love to have named a pup Caterways Very Forward March Chick, but it's just too long. Regretfully I abandoned the scheme.

The alphabet idea didn't appeal to me. I tried once or twice giving names with the same initials as the sire, but this was too restricting. When Sunny had her litter of eleven, all surviving, I thought it was such a good effort that I decided to give them all names beginning with S and found a magnificent list which I could only describe as 'people doing things beginning with S'. A clumsy title, but it was one of my all-time favourite lists – Shoeshiner, Soothsayer, Surfrider, Sharpshooter, Swordfighter, Stargazer, Sightseer, Sandpiper, Sunworshipper, Scenestealer and Spellbinder.

This gave me the idea of choosing a theme for each litter and I have had a lot of fun with it. Three puppies sired by Loudwell Mayboy were my Boy and Girl litter – Cowboy, Choirboy and Countrygirl (Storm). Storm's first litter were all called after her with names like Thunderstorm, Storm of Applause, Stormcrest and Storm in a Teacup. I've had a Christmas litter, a Long Hot Summer litter, a Telephone litter (born on the hundredth anniversary of the first telephone call – and including Smart Operator and Pring Pring). More recently I've had a pop song litter and another named after items of food!

The advantage of some system of group names is that it makes it much easier to identify the puppies should you come across them in later life. Of the dogs I've kept myself my favourite names have been Dreamtime (Socks), Spell-binder (Spangles), Holidaymaker (Saffron) and Sugar Lump (Sugar).

I like my names English, for this is an English breed; unusual; and if possible with a dash of poetry to them. While they must conform to the theme I don't forget that each is going to be a separate name for an individual dog, and if it can't be in some way complimentary I try to make it funny in a kind way so that the owner will be pleased with it.

Another thing which must not be forgotten at this stage is advertising. Unless most of the litter is already booked I like to get my advertisements out by the time the pups are a month old, because they are unlikely to be all snapped up in one week.

Now too the prospective buyers begin turning up to view, often without prior notice. They all want first pick and can be very difficult to convince that they cannot all have it. Then there are those who look at my pile of black babies with the tan paws and say 'We really wanted one with more brown on it like the mother.' And those who insist on coming to view at two or three weeks and decide to go elsewhere because 'We want a bigger one', not being prepared to take my word for it that the pups will grow. And those who literally spend hours 'choosing' their puppy at an age so young that they haven't a snowball's chance in hell of knowing it again at seven weeks, and when I point it out for them decide that they will choose again because the puppies have changed so much.

And all the time my infants are growing and altering. Probably because of my liberal food and freedom regime they always come on very fast at this age. At six weeks they will be given their first dog biscuits, and how they enjoy getting their needle teeth into something solid!

With every week that passes after the sixth a litter of puppies gets more expensive to feed and harder to cope with. Their capacity for food seems to double every few days and their output of waste matter to quadruple. Paws, four per pup and all disproportionately large, seem to be always wet and dirty and to leave as much grime on the walls as on the floor. Needle teeth are busy on everything, from the woodwork of the kennel to the kitchen floorcovering, not forgetting the ears of the other puppies.

If you give them the run of the garden they will reduce it in short order to a miniature Somme, and if you don't watch them they will struggle through the fence and away. At first light they will be awake and yelling in chorus for attention, to the fury of any neighbours within earshot. And if they are not fed last thing at night as well, they won't even wait till daylight. This goes on seven days a week, and in the absence of any firm orders becomes an endurance test both mental and physical.

This at least was my experience with my early litters. Since I seem less beset by these troubles now I think many of them were due to a lack of know-how on my part, but they taught me that breeding is by no means as easy as it seems. Pet people often say 'I couldn't breed because I couldn't bear to part with the puppies.' Well, it isn't quite like that. Half a dozen breathtaking bundles of fluff at three weeks can be six hellhounds at three months who make life such misery for their owners that their departure for pastures new brings nothing but sighs of relief.

I sometimes think that puppies would be much improved if they had no teeth! In my heroic attempts to induce mental and physical soundness in my babies I have bitten on the bullet repeatedly to assuage my anguish at the destruction of a favourite shrub, the ruin of new vinyl floor covering, the stripping of wallpaper, the chewing of rugs.

But far the worst use of their teeth is when they use them on each other. Your average Airedale puppy loves a fight, but mostly it is a harmless cowboys and Indians affair indulged in without malice and enjoyed by all participants. What usually happens is that Pup A pounces on Pup B, bears him to the ground and sinks his teeth joyfully into his prey. Pup B promptly squeals at the top of his voice. This surprises Pup A, who lets go and looks round to see where the noise is coming from, giving Pup B a chance to escape, and incidentally forgetting that he was having a fight in the first place. Pup B gets away and they both do something else and all is well.

But now and then you get a litter in which Pup B will be silent under attack. There is nothing to put Pup A off his stroke so Pup B loses his temper and retaliates. Neither will let go and often other puppies join in. Since all this is done in silence the hapless breeder has no idea that anything is wrong until she goes to the run and finds it full of puppies lying shocked and soaked with saliva. Although actual wounds are seldom visible if often happens that the punctures caused by piercing with eye teeth become infected and nasty abscesses result.

I never had a fighting litter until Chai had her seven puppies. I thought it must have been caused by Chai's peculiarly antagonistic attitude to her children, aggravated by the cold and inhospitable conditions in which I was forced to house them to keep them out of her way. This may have been a contributory factor, but I have had several instances since when none of these conditions were present, and I have been forced to the conclusion that it just depends on how the puppies are. Some litters do seem to bite far harder than others, but generally I find that if they yell under attack they will be all right. If they don't then we are all in for trouble.

After due thought I noticed that my puppies tended to fight when two particular strains were present in their pedigrees. I don't blame either strain, but believe the trouble only arose when both combined. I abandoned this combination and the trouble stopped, but I abandoned it with regret because these puppies did not grow up to be fighters. On the contrary they were gentle, obedient and good looking and gave great pleasure to their owners, but rearing them in the litter stage was a nightmare which just got to be too much for me.

I don't want to give the impression that this is a vice of this breed alone. On the contrary I have heard of puppies in some breeds actually killing each other, but I have never heard of such a thing in Airedales; and a breeder of another variety of whom I asked advice was surprised that I didn't always separate my pups at five weeks as he did.

Airedale puppies can also be too ready to use their teeth

on their human companions. This is always done in fun but can be a nuisance if not checked. And every one without exception could get his school certificate in undoing shoelaces without ever having a single lesson on the subject!

18

Ready to be sold

As my puppies are always well advanced by seven weeks, this is the age from which I sell them. I don't say that this should be the same for every breed (some smaller breeds I am sure are better kept a week or so longer) but with my Airedales I believe that after seven weeks they are better in every way in a good caring home. Physically they bloom and mentally their characters and brains develop in a quite astonishing way.

This is not to say that selling doesn't present problems. Not the problem of finding a buyer and getting your money, but the far more difficult one of finding buyers good enough to be entrusted with your puppies, and matching your puppies to the homes offered. I'm not the only breeder who immediately feels antagonistic to the voice on the phone which says 'I see you're advertising puppies', although I don't go as far as one I know who becomes positively rude in an attempt to put her would-be customers off altogether.

When I take an enquiry on the telephone I am listening hard to the voice, trying to assess the personality behind it. It's a help but it's not infallible. It is impossible to really sort out one's impression of a buyer in a telephone conversation, but when one has invited them to come and see the puppies, they naturally expect to be able to buy if they like what they see. If you don't like what *you* see it is very difficult indeed to refuse, especially if they have come a long way, but there are times when this must be done. When this happens I try to emphasise that a mistaken purchase will certainly bring trouble, worry and expense to the owner as well as unhappiness to the dog.

I like best the people who have had an Airedale before. They know what they are taking on and must understand the breed if they want to repeat the dose. Worst of all are the finicky over-particular people. They are continually pushing the dogs away and brushing off their clothes, and like the people who are constantly demanding minute details of feeding, training, etc., give me no confidence in their ability to cope successfully with so much abounding life and joy as is contained in the average Airedale pup.

One rule I am strict on – never knowingly to sell a puppy to a home where it will be left alone all day. Dogs are pack animals and it is sheer cruelty to condemn them to a life of solitary confinement, especially when young. Some older dogs who are set in their habits do adapt quite well to such a life, but even they would be happier with someone about the house during the day. I remember the case of a small poodle who had such a fate, shut in the kitchen for nine hours a day six days a week. Her owner protested that she had everything she needed and was 'perfectly happy'. This went on for years until a married daughter with a baby moved in pending the finding of a new house.

The daughter was there for six months and nobody apparently noticed any change in the dog. But when the day came that the house was found and the poor little thing resumed her life in 'solitary' they found a sad difference then. For the first time in her life she had experienced normal companionship and she just could not resign herself to a resumption of the starved existence she had known too well. First she howled, then she became dirty in the house and at last her mind became affected and she had to be put down – a merciful release in my opinion. Her owner said it would never have happened if Anne hadn't moved in. Probably not; the dog would have gone on in her pathetic half-life for many more dismal years.

I do sympathise with anyone who feels the need for a dog, but if they are really dog lovers they will realise they are being selfish. They will all tell you that the dog is perfectly happy – so it is while they are there to see it, sometimes wildly happy on the rebound from its day of misery. I have had a number of 'absentee owners' in my trimming business. They leave a key where I can find it, or in some cases they give me a key of my own so that I can let myself in to do my stuff. I go in to a startled and timid dog, surprised out of its lonesome trance, who tries frantically to escape me. You should try winkling a terrified poodle out from between the sheets of someone's bed in a deserted house.

But when the trim has been accomplished, the bag packed and the hair swept tidily into the dustpan, what a heartbroken howling follows me down the garden path. The dog's solitude has been breached, its resistance overcome, the ordeal of the trim is over, and how bitterly its desolation settles back on it as it realises that it is once more alone in the dead empty house, all silent except for the sad sounds of the fridge humming and the thermostat clicking now and then on the boiler. That's not for my puppies if I can possibly avoid it.

Insisting on homes 'with company' automatically means that you must sell to a lot of people with young children. Some breeders don't like this, and it is understandable especially where small breeds are concerned. Children can be quite merciless even in their affections, and parents can be amazingly obtuse.

I remember being called in to administer its first trim to a minute toy poodle puppy no bigger than a kitten, and being horrified to find it being carried around the house by several young children who were quarrelling as to who should have it. It was in a coma of exhaustion, a fact quite unnoticed by the doting mother, who had only felt pleased at the amount it would stand without biting its tormentors. She seemed surprised but not particularly worried when I pointed out its condition, so I told her it might go into fits and die if it wasn't allowed the sleep all babies need. I don't know or care if this was true; it pulled Mama up short, and the poor mite was given some peace.

A breeder once received a phone call from an owner complaining that the bitch he had bought as a puppy had begun growling at the children. As it was then three years old she asked in what circumstances it was doing this.

'When they stand on her' was the reply!

After pointing out that not only was the bitch getting old enough to begin wanting a bit of peace and quiet, but also that children get a lot heavier in three years, the breeder pointed out with some heat that so far from complaining about the dog's temperament, the owner should congratulate himself that she was only growling and not biting. He seemed surprised by this line of thought. 'What do you advise then?' he asked, and received in ringing tones the reply 'Start training your (asterisk) kids!'

Personally I don't object to my puppies going where there are children as long as I like the adults. Airedales love kids and in that dangerous second six months of the dog's life it is often only the children's love and insistence which keeps the adolescent hellhound in the family. But I do tell the parents in the plainest terms that whatever John or Julia may promise, the work and responsibility for the pup will inevitably fall on them. There may be one child in a thousand capable of keeping those promises, but that's probably putting it rather high.

Like all conscientious breeders I have learnt to respect the rule never to push a sale. The odds against a 'persuaded' sale turning out well are too heavy, even when the persuasion only concerns such particulars as age, sex or breed. Let the buyer choose whether to buy. If he buys, let him choose what to buy. But you're always at liberty to refuse!

Refusing isn't all that easy, though, because every

would-be buyer bar none is one hundred per cent positive that in the words of the song 'The doggy would have a good home.'

For my own pups I know that very many of them are far better off than they would be with me. There are the dogs who go away with their owners every weekend, perhaps caravanning or sailing, or to their owners' own holiday cottage. Or the two who have been trained to the gun and given the freedom of four hundred acres, for instance, and many other pets who just live in luxury with their every need carefully and lovingly supplied. Not that money is everything: my dog-fixated Bermondsey childhood taught me that.

My own Airedales are healthy and happy. I keep them so at some sacrifice to myself, and am more than repaid by their being such a pleasure to live with. But I don't delude myself into thinking that *no one* can provide a better home.

A young Airedale needs love. It needs an outlet for its high spirits and a kind and firm discipline. It needs the run of a garden which is properly fenced and the freedom of the family's living rooms so that it will settle into an affectionate and enjoyable family dog. These are simple precepts. It is surprising how many people fall down on them!

The point about fencing is that the Airedale is both inquisitive and a hunter. His nose follows a tempting scent, the rest of him goes with it, and if he is not checked he will become a roamer. Patching up holes in the fence will merely act as a challenge. He will get cleverer and cleverer each time he escapes, and more and more expensive measures will have to be taken in the attempt to keep him in.

This happened to a bitch I sold to a young lady some years ago. Once Nancy had been down to the river and slaughtered her first rat nothing could stop her, until in desperation a considerable sum was spent on solid wood fencing. But somehow Miss Nancy still got out. Her owner hit on the plan of leaving the back door ajar and running upstairs to a window to watch, for no self-respecting Airedale will betray its escape routes if it knows

186

it is being watched.

It worked. Out came Nancy, coolly trotted over to an apple tree and scrambled on to a branch from whence she was able to jump across the fence! This sort of thing is the culmination of long practice in escaping which has sharpened the ingenuity. If the pup is surrounded by a good fence *from the start* it will accept it as one of the facts of life and not try to get out, making its owners' life much easier and its own much safer.

Some people believe that if a dog means to get out it will, no matter what is done to stop it. I don't agree with this, but after my apprenticeship with Toffee I understand the problem and one certainly needs a lot of luck if the dog is to be kept from harm while one is struggling to achieve a dogproof garden.

Poor Teddy, one of my puppies, was tragically killed one morning while trying to reach a nearby bitch in season. Certainly no blame attached to his owners, who had done so much to prevent such an escape and were absolutely stricken by their loss. In fact his mistress sent me a beautiful bunch of chrysanthemums with a message thanking me for 'two years of a wonderful dog'. That any owner of a dog bred by me should feel like that about him means far more to me than any show honours ever could, for if a dog is not a joy to live with, what good is it if it is beautiful?

One of the nicest things about dog breeding is that among the buyers of each litter one will almost always become a friend. Teddy's Mum sent me flowers, Nancy's Mum asks me to lunch, Candy's Mum became a breeder herself and one of my greatest friends, and so it goes on. When that phone rings one never knows what may be beginning.

It rang one evening and a voice asked me desperately if I had a bitch for sale. As it happened I had just one, much to my caller's relief, for she told me that she had never been without an Airedale bitch from the day she was born until the day before her call, when her last one had died suddenly after a collapse. She had rung twenty-seven breeders all over England before getting my name, and not one of them had a bitch puppy available! I described Shanty to her and she asked me if I would send her up to Yorkshire by air. I did this and Shanty's new owners were at the airport to meet her. They thought she would be terrified by her journey and turned up equipped with brandy, hot water bottles and the *best* pink Witney blankets with which to comfort her should she be in a state of shock! But to their delight, on being released from her travelling box, Shanty kissed the airport official on the nose and looked round her as one who would say 'Well, I'm here, where's the cameras?'

Soon I began to get letters and photographs to illustrate Shanty's progress, and often there were invitations to go and visit, taking all the 'girls'. I accepted. What sort of heroes let themselves in for a week's visit from a woman they have never seen, accompanied by four adult and unknown Airedale bitches? They were absolutely charming and genuinely delighted to meet us all. 'Everywhere you look there's an Airedale,' chuckled Shanty's dad, and thought it wonderful.

I found that they lived in an old cottage with walls two feet thick, high over Wharfedale, with a long terraced garden running right down the hill. My dogs thought it heaven, and I'm glad to say behaved pretty well. Every day they hunted rabbits by the river, watched with some contempt by Shanty, who knew perfectly well that they were all among the brambles on the hill. She must be one of the luckiest dogs alive.

But a pup not so lucky was one I sold to what should have been the perfect home. Charming people with a lovely house and an acre of garden, and best of all, Airedale owners of long standing. All the reports I got of Bruce were most glowing, and especially did his mistress praise his wonderful nature. She often said that he was not only the handsomest Airedale they had ever had, but that he possessed far and away the best temperament – not surprising as he was one of Bamu's sons. When he was about eighteen months I went to their home to trim him. He certainly was beautiful and I was quite thrilled with him, but uneasy when his mistress told me that he had recently been within a whisker of being put down for total and persistent eczema. He certainly had the run of the garden, by the way, but in spite of his lovely character was only allowed in the house as far as the kitchen.

On this visit I met the two children for the first time. Of course it can't be an infallible rule, but I have usually found that people can be judged by their offspring, and I have seldom disliked children more than I did these. Nor was I better pleased with them when their mother praised the dog for his endurance without retaliation under the children's teasing.

Things went on like this, with Bruce continually suffering terrible attacks of wet eczema until one day when he was four years old his owners asked me to find a home for him as they were emigrating. Fortunately I was able to place him with a young couple. His new circumstances might have seemed a change for the worse as they had no garden but lived in a flat over a shop. But they were thrilled with their beautiful acquisition.

No more being kept in the kitchen. Where his new owners lived, he lived. They took him to parties, they took him on holiday. When their children arrived they moved to a house by the sea and he went with them. And they told me that when they first went to collect him from his old home he went with them without a backward glance, and most significant of all, he never had another attack of eczema!

It had obviously been a nervous eczema brought on by the relentless teasing of those horrible children. Many people seem completely unable to understand that teasing is a form of torture to a sensitive dog, and since then I always point it out to puppy buyers with young children, and impress on them that it is real cruelty and has no place in a Good Home.

A good home! One of the earliest stumbling blocks novice breeders must overcome is the belief that no one else can give these little darlings such a good home as they can. In fact lots don't overcome it, which naturally means the end of their career as breeders. I knew the owner of a pomeranian who was quite unable to part with its two daughters. Three poms are rather a nice idea, but what a good job they were all bitches!

Personally I am only too anxious to see the last of my pups by the time they are old enough to go, as by then I am worn to a rag and slowly going out of my mind. But that doesn't make me any less choosy when it comes to sorting out their new owners, and if I don't approve it's no sale. As in the case of the voice on the phone which said it hadn't time to come in person but would send one of its lorry drivers to collect a puppy. Bristling but cunning I asked more questions and eventually the voice said frankly that the pup was wanted as a replacement for a bull terrier which had been put down after savaging a little girl who had wandered into the yard where it was chained up. That was enough. I told him politely that I was sorry but my puppies were not suitable for such a life as they were bred and reared to be family dogs and house companions, not yard dogs.

The most difficult people to refuse are those who sound all right on the phone but to whom you take a dislike when they arrive on your doorstep. You have perhaps only a nebulous feeling that all is not right. Can you allow people to come perhaps over a hundred miles for a puppy and then refuse them in spite of their credentials being in order? Fenced garden, intelligent people, wife at home all day, good area for dogs, money no object – when the only reason you can give is:

> *I do not like thee, Doctor Fell,*
> *The reason why I cannot tell?*

But the only puppy I ever sold which to my knowledge had a miserable life and came to a bad and premature end was sold in just such a sale. I blame myself bitterly, because a few days after he was sold his new owner phoned to say that although a super puppy he was continually crying and howling even when they were with him. In fact I could hear him over the phone. I had him back for a week, when he immediately became his old cheeky self. What I should have done was to insist on hav-

190

ing him back for good, subsequent events proving only too well that in that particular home he was a square peg in a round hole.

However I did learn the lesson and now always try to reclaim misfit puppies. In another case the pup was brought back by his new owners, who had been unable to make him eat in the four days they had had him. I had a large meal ready for him, and after greeting me rapturously he put his head and both front feet into the bowl and smartly wolfed the lot, subsequently washing it down with a long drink of milk.

It wasn't a case of Dr Fell here. It soon transpired that the pup had been bought as a last resource by this couple who were unable to have the child they so desired. But the little chap's refusal to eat had so affected his new mistress that she developed guilt feelings because she was expending so much anxiety and mental anguish on a dog instead of a child. I've no doubt this nervous tension had affected the puppy in turn and prolonged the resistance to food, Airedales being extremely sensitive to this sort of stress.

I was only too glad to refund them their money (unasked) and retain small Billy. The person I felt sorriest for was the husband, who now had to renounce a dog which he had fallen for very heavily. He begged me not to blame the puppy as he believed it would be impossible ever to meet with his equal, and they could see from his altered appetite and behaviour since his return that it was their fault and not his if he had not felt happy in his new home.

I don't blame myself for this sale as I liked this couple and felt very sorry for them. The Dr Fells are different, like the family who arrived in force to inspect my wares all impeccably dressed as for a High School prizegiving. The wife had a wondrous hat, a virgin white suit, sheerest stockings and patent leather court shoes. She was horrified by the enthusiastic scrabblings threatened by the puppies and kept well out of reach. The children said not a word. They appeared pessimistic but dutiful. Casting about for an excuse to say No I was delighted when Mother said that their last dog had been a Maltese and that was what they really wanted but had been unable to find. I firmly read them a lecture on the inadvisability of going into a different breed when you had found the one which really suited you. This was well received, possibly even with relief, and I packed them off happily with the address of a good Maltese breeder who usually had puppies for sale.

In most Doctor Fell cases, however, there is no such excuse readily provided. Now I have become sufficiently brazen to say firmly that I believe their home and my puppy to be unsuited to each other. Without actually saying they can't have him I paint a black picture of their future together and stress the expense to them in peace of mind, trouble, time, carpets, furniture, garden, noise and above all money, if they are so foolish as to persist in letting themselves in for it. I then suggest they go home and think about it. So far it has always worked. Not one of them has so much as rung back to say they have changed their minds.

I can imagine them telling their friends about this peculiar woman who breeds and advertises puppies and then won't sell them. I don't mind. Every dog breeder worth her salt that I know of has her eccentricities and I know I've got mine – although I don't consider vetting of would-be purchasers to be one of them.

One of the oddest visits from prospective buyers came when I was selling Bamu's first litter and was still very green. Two middle-aged women turned up to view the goods. They were large and plump. Their clothes were better than their accents and their eyes were hard. My puppies did look rather gorgeous that day. We had made them a pen on the lawn beneath some trees and filled it with fresh golden straw, and they were all lively, well grown and active. The visitors were rendered quite speechless by their beauty and spent half an hour exclaiming in admiration.

No doubt about a sale here, I thought – I was still in the does-nobody-want-my-beautiful-puppies stage – but they made no choice and produced no money. At last I was constrained to ask them which one they wanted. They drew back in apparent pain. Oh no, they couldn't think of buying one of those puppies. They only wanted a pet, but they did know BREED when they saw it, and it would be sacrilege to waste one of those puppies on a pet home. They should all go where they could be shown and take their rightful places in the world. Completely astonished I tried to inject some sort of reason into this specious rubbish. No good, they positively refused to shell out and take one of these paragons off my hands!

They quite took my breath away, but the reason for their refusal became apparent when I looked through the local newspaper. In spite of the fact that Airedales were still almost never advertised, there was a second litter – and not far away. I'm quite sure that these oddly behaved women were the breeders who had simply come to weigh up the opposition.

I suppose that my favourite customers are still the Yorkshire couple who took Shanty and made her so happy. Some customers are terrible timewasters and seem to think that anyone with puppies has nothing to do. They are the bane of all breeders, who never have enough time even for essentials. I personally don't mind the buyers who ask if they can come several times to see the puppies. Such people are usually keen and considerate and it is good to know that they are so eager to get to know the pups, and when they eventually collect their puppy it will not be going to complete strangers.

Children brought by parents to choose a puppy can be a menace. Personally I don't think children should be allowed to choose anything so important.

I had an extreme case of this when a lady rang to make an appointment to see the puppies. She sounded excited and confessed that she had always longed for an Airedale but that it had never before been possible. A few days later she rang again to cancel the order. Her nine-year-old daughter had gone to a friend's house and seen a litter of a much smaller and notoriously nervy breed and that was that. Mother was disappointed to the point of tears, but Daughter's word was law.

I just can't see that the choice of the breed of the family dog is the child's prerogative. Would these parents extend the same privilege to their infants in the choice of the make and model of the family car? I very much doubt it, yet the dog is likely to be with them much longer than the car.

This child of course I never met, but I've met plenty! It is astonishing how quickly a small child's interest in puppies evaporates. Long before his parents have finished asking questions the little darlings are finding other means of passing the time, like jumping off my flower border to the drive beneath or going round opening cupboards and drawers, or asking loudly 'Hasn't this lady got any cake?'

One learns the hard way. After a fourteen-year-old infant was found upstairs sitting on my bed talking to my dogs, and a five year old ditto had come down with some ornaments from my dressing table, I constructed a light wire gate to fix across the bottom of the stairs. One small boy, tugging and shaking at this like an all-in wrestler, asked me 'What's this for?'

I replied casually but with inward glee, 'To stop you going upstairs.'

'Why?' – indignantly.

'Because it's private up there.'

Dumbfounded looks from both mother and son, but the gate-shaking stopped. Another two converts to the 'peculiar woman' school of thought.

I try to keep in touch with as many of my puppies as I can after selling them, and hear a good many funny stories.

It is very common for Airedale puppies to lose interest in food on first going to new homes. This is mainly due to missing the competition with its litter mates which results in a mad rush for the trough, but no doubt strangeness, homesickness and the need to absorb new impressions all play their part. This soon wears off as a rule, but sometimes does persist especially if the owners become too worried and try to tempt it with hand-fed dainties.

This was the case with Jack, the newest member of a very jolly family. He refused his dinner one Sunday just as the family were about to sit down to theirs.

'Perhaps he wants the same as us,' said Mum, so

194

scraped out his dish and refilled it with food from the table.

'No thank you,' said Jack.

'He doesn't like his dish, give him a plate like ours,' said the children. Jack sniffed at the plate with its tempting load, hesitated, and then –

'No thank you,' said Jack.

'Dash it all,' burst out Dad in exasperation, 'I suppose you want a knife and fork now!' and put them down on either side of the plate on the carpet.

'That's better!' said Jack. And cleared the lot!'

There are the naughty stories too, which usually provoke more laughter than wrath.

Such as that of the much adored ten month old Casey, who on being let out into the garden one bright spring morning found a gate not properly latched and went out on his own.

Great fun, thought Casey, and began to explore lawns and shrubberies at top speed. Unluckily his attention was drawn to the garden next door, and right away he found the back door open. Still in top gear he shot through it and dashed into the dining room, where the old lady who lived there was just sitting down to her lunch.

Quick as lightning Casey swiped the pork chop from her plate just as she was about to stick her fork in it – and was gone.

His owner, who hadn't even realised that he wasn't in his own garden, was astonished to see him coming in via the front gate. She saw that he had something in his mouth and took it away, mentally cursing the person so stupid as to give him a chop bone. It wasn't till the following day that another neighbour told her what had happened, when she returned the chop in triplicate together with abject apologies. Fortunately the old lady took it well. Although annoyed at the time, reflection had shown her that she herself was partly to blame since when Casey was small she had encouraged him to come in and had always fed him.

But this escapade pales into insignificance beside that of Iris, a bitch puppy with shades of Toffee about her. She

195

had shot up in height so that at nine months she was already a very tall Airedale, dressed in a gleaming coat of brilliant black trimmed with bright gold. She was absolutely tireless but nevertheless stood very high in her owner's opinion.

One day this lady and three friends decided to take their four dogs for a run on the common. This was the usual stretch of rough grassland bordered by woods, pleasant enough in summer, but only frequented by dogs and maniacs in bad weather. On this occasion there had been a good deal of rain, so they dressed in the appropriate (or tramps') gear, ie gumboots, old slacks and shabby coats. The dogs were let loose to play, the humans chatted peacefully of this and that, and everyone was happy until they saw coming towards them a woman who was definitely *not* dressed for the occasion.

Her hair was tastefully arranged beneath a silk head-square, she wore a three-quarter length coat, the finest of stockings and immaculate high-heeled shoes. She was leading a bored golden Afghan hound on a blue lead, and her nose was in the air.

Iris's owner swears that this vision would not have condescended to acknowledge their existence had it not been for Iris, who happened to be the only pure bred dog of the four. Ignoring the three little mongrels, the woman swished up to Iris, and in a very affected voice gushed 'What a divine little Airedale!' and bent over to pat her on the head.

How thoughtlessly do we all perform these trivial acts, casual and carefree, reckless of what events may lie in the womb of time. Had she known much about Airedales she surely would have known one of the cardinal facts about the breed, which is that nine month old puppies seldom miss a chance.

Iris certainly didn't. The kindest thing we can say is that she made a grab for the bright silk square, but if that was her object she missed it sensationally and connected instead with the quiff of hair in front. The woman screamed, Iris tugged, and before the horrified onlookers could make a move she was away – triumphantly bearing the woman's hairpiece!

Now Iris's mistress had been training her conscientiously and usually had no difficulty in getting her to come, but this was another ball game altogether. Or wig game. For Iris was over the moon with her unexpected booty and had no intention of surrendering it. For twenty-five long minutes the four perspiring friends panted after her while she ran, spun, leaped and had high jinks generally with her trophy. She tossed it into the air, and when it dropped into muddy puddles raked it out gaily with her foot. Once when the hunt came a little too near she was seen to run into the wood and bury it among the tree roots. Realising that this ploy had been spotted by the hunters she deftly disinterred it and bolted before they got to her.

All this time the four were studiously averting their eyes from each other, knowing that if once they met the chase would disintegrate into mass hysteria. As Iris's owner put it, it wouldn't have been half so funny – 'and we did feel sorry for her, it was an awful thing to happen, but if she hadn't been so snooty we would have been much less amused and more sympathetic.'

The bereaved woman was understandably furious, and when her bedraggled crowning glory was at last restored to her, said a few trenchant words about dogs being trained to come when they were called. This provoked one of the friends to ask sweetly whether that was why she kept her Afghan on the lead, knowing well that this breed is notorious for running off.

Iris's owner offered her name and address and full restitution, but outraged dignity would not allow its acceptance, and the woman stalked off with the depressed Afghan. I wonder whether she told the story to her friends, and if so what their reaction was? Probably she decided that the wisest course was to suffer in silence.

19

You don't see many of those about nowadays

Although this is not meant to be an Airedale book, as my favourite breed they inevitably figure largely in its pages, and therefore it might not be out of place to include a few words on the breed itself.

For years people have been telling me that 'you don't see many of those about nowadays' – a remark which may be true for them but certainly not for me! After the war Airedale numbers certainly declined to a very low ebb, nevertheless good puppies have always sold, and after Ch.Riverina Tweedsbairn went Best in Show at Crufts in 1961 a revival began, almost imperceptible at first, but gradually increasing until now it is not too much to say that the breed is booming.

The Airedale is a breed which was deliberately manufactured by a group of Yorkshire businessmen in the midnineteenth century. It was not, as many think, a miners' dog like the whippet; in fact it originated in a part of the county where little or no mining was done, near Bingley.

At first it was called the Bingley terrier, and other names were the Waterside terrier or broken-haired terrier, but eventually its creators settled on the lovely name Airedale as expressive of the whole area from which it sprang.

These gentlemen were trying to produce a strong sporting terrier capable of hunting with Otterhounds, going to ground in the otter's holt, and drawing the quarry out. It needed to be larger than the other terriers then in use, to be very courageous, to have a first-class nose and to be a strong swimmer.

They succeeded in all these aims and must have been well satisfied with their new terrier, for all their breeding records were then destroyed so that nobody else could copy their matings. This has inevitably left some uncertainty as to the ingredients used. Although some have suggested the Foxhound as a likely ancestor the Otterhound is the one most usually accepted, and this breed could have contributed size, strength, scenting and swimming powers and also the black and tan or grizzle colouring and the rough broken coat. Some sort of terrier was also used, some say the Old English terrier, a white breed now extinct but from which all terrier breeds are believed to stem.

Personally I am always intrigued by Emily Bronte's drawing of her dog Grasper, a black and tan mongrel terrier with quite a strong look of an old-fashioned Airedale with very sparse whiskers and beard. I don't suggest that this dog was actually used in the manufacture of the Airedale, but I think it likely that he was typical of a strain of local terrier which may very well have been common in the area. After all Haworth is not far from Bingley, and the dates are near enough. It's quite possible that one of Grasper's relatives took the eye of those Yorkshire pioneers and played his part in their plans!

Another job the Airedale was designed for was ridding the district of polecats. I imagine he went at this task with enthusiasm: at any rate the polecats disappeared. I have had several ill-advised ferrets killed by my own dogs when straying across my garden, so I can vouch at first hand for their aptitude in dealing with this type of rodent.

Other breeds must also have played their part in making the Airedale, and among those suggested have been the bull terrier, curly coated retriever, collie and Old English sheepdog. Whatever the recipe – and there are even today many quite distinct types of Airedale – the result must have surpassed all expectations.

He has proved his worth not only as a sporting terrier. The French value him as a gundog, the Japanese as a police dog. He has been trained to guide the blind and is a superb guard and housedog. When kept as a family dog he has the advantage that if properly looked after his coat does not shed indoors and he is very little troubled by hereditary diseases. He is clean in his habits, friendly and outgoing in his nature and good with children. Excitable but not hysterical, playful but not restless, he knows how to be quiet and make himself scarce in the house, yet he is always ready for anything.

He is quick to learn, quick to understand human speech. He never forgets a friend yet he very seldom remembers a grudge. He is not over-aggressive, over-possessive, or jealous. He can be stubborn but he is very sensitive and affectionate, which means that he will not respond to browbeating but will do anything for love. He can certainly be naughty and he is the most inquisitive dog on earth.

As the decades have passed he has become more and more handsome, and it is a serious responsibility to breeders in achieving this not to lose the unique character which makes him not only the King of Terriers as he is called, but supreme among dogs. Any breed can be beautiful, but only one can have the true Airedale nature, warm, humorous and true.

In the 1914–18 war, Col. E. Richardson trained a number of Airedales as messengers to work in the front line, and in peace he was famous for his guard dogs. He believed the Airedale was particularly suited for this work in this country because his ability to distinguish between strangers and the members of staff of even the largest households made him much safer to use than less discriminating breeds.

However, any Airedale simply kept chained up will become vicious. The cruelty and inactivity forced on such active and mentally alert dogs does eventually unhinge their minds and in their misery they become dangerous. Also, although Airedales seldom feel the cold they do suffer from the heat, and for these two reasons I am glad that they are not often kept as guards now, except in the domestic sense as free-running and valued members of their owners' families.

It is a very happy thing to have found 'your' breed, for it is a possession which can never be taken from you. I always say that no one knows what an Airedale can be who has not lived with one. He is a dog to warm your heart, with the humour and playfulness which he never outgrows, his gentleness, his rowdiness, his nosiness, his reasonableness, his facility for understanding and all but uttering speech. For me he is among the necessities of life.

PART FOUR
Training

Working at Crufts

In unison they move away,
Tracing a pattern on the floor.
This is their summit, now, today,
The crown of all they've laboured for.
Handler and dog, absorbed, intent,
Tread through the Heelwork minuet
Like dancers, till their time is spent
And motionless they stand once more.

Full marks! The steward lifts his hands,
Stilling the ringside's ready roar.

Dreamlike they work, and like a dream
Such skilled perfection is to me.
Crufts, with its champions supreme,
Will not, I fear, my triumphs see.
But yet I toil as best I can
To reconcile two distant worlds,
That mind of dog and mind of man
May know each other's mystery.

This is a dream I can achieve,
Good dog, good friend, good company.

20
Who else?

Guess who was responsible for me joining a training club and discovering the whole world of dog Obedience? You're right, who else but Toffee, the first dog I ever had that I couldn't manage without assistance.

Toffee was two and a half and I felt we were at a crisis, mutually loving yet unable either to part or to live together, when another Airedale owner suggested that I took her to the local dogs' Borstal. I didn't even know it existed.

I had seen a short article in the paper soon after the war in which it announced the proposed setting up of classes and asked for people with doggy experience to make contact with the organisers, who if I remember rightly were the Kennel Club. I wanted very much to volunteer then, but my husband vetoed the idea and to my lasting regret I was thus prevented from being in Obedience from the very beginning.

Now I jumped at the suggestion and rang the local club

Chairman for particulars. The Chairman turned out to be a very charming woman who listened patiently to my tale of woe, which I realised later she must have heard many times, though not often, I suspect, with such good reason. She kindly encouraged me by saying that many equally difficult dogs had become reformed characters after a few months attendance at this college.

Still convinced that Toffee was untrainable I nevertheless turned up on the next club night after walking from home, which took me three quarters of an hour. Toffee had had her usual exercise, food, etc., but this didn't stop her from enjoying this refreshing stroll, and she arrived much brighter and more alert than I did.

I took a deep breath and an iron grip on the lead before entering the shabby old church hall where it was all happening. Just as well, as it seemed to be full of dogs of all sorts and the noise was deafening. Oddly enough the only dog I really remember at all from that first night was a coal black working collie of sorts with blazing eyes, flaring prick ears and a vast expanse of scarlet tongue and gums, bordered by a palisade of enormous white teeth. This latter ensemble was much in evidence, since what time he could spare from panting he utilized in producing an horrific barrage of barking and screaming – in fact the major part of that appalling racket was his contribution.

Toffee was beside herself with joy. She thought it was the biggest, jolliest and certainly the loudest party she had ever been to, and was all eagerness to get in there and join the fun.

The Chairman, the lady who had spoken to me on the phone, was there and had a few kind words to say to me and tactfully admired my heaving incubus. She had two daughters with her and they all had Welsh Corgis, then at the zenith of their popularity. There were several instructors, including an Air Force type known as Doug who followed me out as I was leaving to say he hoped I would come again, and how rare it was to see an Airedale in training. He seemed to think Toff would be an acquisition to the club. I silently pitied his ignorance on this last point but was grateful for the feeling of friendliness and welcome which this conversation conveyed.

There was also a girl working a Lakeland terrier in the Advanced class. The smart results she got out of this little dog left me gasping, and I felt quite flattered when she sat beside me, admired Toff and said how nice it would be to have another terrier in the club. We are both members still and have been friends ever since that night.

Toffee's behaviour in class was quite predictable. Elated, absorbed, transfigured, she dragged me from side to side relentlessly and spent the entire evening trying to fraternise with her fellow members. Oblivious of any commands I might be uttering, she had a whale of a time. But in spite of all she could do, and although I tottered home feeling as if I had first been under a steam roller and then mangled, the bug had bitten. In fact I was a serious case, and whether Toff ever learnt a single thing or not, I knew that wild horses couldn't have kept me away after that first night.

To be among people who felt much as I did about dogs was like emerging from a strange land into a country where everyone spoke a language I knew.

I even suspected (or was I imagining it?) that Toffee was just a shade more tractable on the way home. She may have been, for early training classes often have an exhausting effect on newly enrolled dogs and they can be quite subdued even for a day or two afterwards. I think it is partly because the excitement of a class makes everything else an anticlimax, and partly because the dog has exercised his brain harder than ever before, and his brain needs exercise as much as any other part.

Next day the family wanted to know all about it, and before long the children wanted to come too. Nor was it long before Stephen demanded to handle his own dog and was enrolled as a junior member. He had already formed that opinion of me as a very poor handler which he has not recanted to this day, but I didn't mind as it enabled me to take Bamu instead, with whom I thought I could get much further.

Stephen certainly had his hands full. During his first class Toffee, instead of sitting beside him on the Halt, threw herself full length on the floor and rolled on to her back. Steve tried to manhandle her into the correct position, but was very properly checked by Doug, who was taking the class.

Taking the lead into his own hands, Doug proceeded to demonstrate.

'If your dog lies down don't pull him up with your hands,' he said kindly, 'but say Heel and step forward. As the dog gets up to follow you, wait till he's got up as far as the Sit position then step smartly back beside him and praise him.'

Doug in his innocence then attempted to show how this method worked, and it worked very well except for one thing. When it came to getting up, Toff, who had obviously been listening, got up back end first, like a cow! End of demonstration.

Bamu, who was four and a half when she started training, came on well. Her intelligence and wish to please me combined to make her a dog whom I could really enjoy training. I had only to explain to her what I wanted her to do – although explaining might take weeks, and sometimes months – and she would do it with pleasure. She was therefore very reliable and it was seldom that she failed to complete an exercise once she had mastered it.

Where Bamu failed was on her slowness and inaccuracy. If I sent her to retrieve she would fumble the pick-up, drop the article on the way back and return so slowly that only repeated commands and encouragement from me (at the top of my voice) would keep her going until she had covered the whole distance. She then usually presented the article without dropping it so long as I wasn't too slow in taking it from her, but couldn't have cared less whether she was sitting straight or even on the prescribed spot, and her 'finish' was equally woolly. As for her Heelwork, this really exhausted me, as it was only by flogging myself to death with extra commands and encouraging signals that I kept her going at all. In spite of this I felt Bamu was not being given full credit for her achievements.

We had a trainer at that time who was very show-minded and didn't seem to have a lot of interest in any dog that wasn't an Alsatian or Border collie and therefore likely to be capable of bringing glory on the club. He arranged a competition night one week in which our hall was thrown open to entrants from other clubs. Show competition was then just beginning to get into its stride and beginning to exert an hypnotic power over the minds of its devotees. Sadly, some dogs were little more than sacrifices to this Moloch, and were not infrequently disposed of when they failed to come up to expectations.

I am glad to say that Obedience has become better understood since then and far more importance is placed on the dog's mental state, as this is really what makes or mars a champion. Long training sessions are also no longer de rigeur and you can believe that owner of the Crufts winner who tells the interviewer that she only spends a few minutes a day training her superdog. Training is now seen more as a matter of upbringing, of training in domestic manners and habits which may well contribute to show performance, and of discouraging traits which may spoil any exercises in the dog's later career.

Also there are now kennels specialising in producing stock for Obedience, and a puppy bought from such a place and reared judiciously by a knowledgeable and skilful handler is half trained before it ever sees the inside of its first training class.

But this is a digression. To get back to that competition night, I decided to enter Bamu in Test B. As this is the second highest test, only Test C being more advanced, you might say I was sticking my neck out, especially as exercises in the two top classes are required to be done on one command only, all extra commands or signals being severely penalised.

The judge's eyes nearly popped out when I began bowling round the ring with much thigh-slapping, praise and murmured endearments to keep my entrant still moving. And that's how we went on, dropping points by the bucketful for extra commands, but Bamu was still awake when Heelwork was finished. Then came the Retrieve, not too bad apart from the inevitable loss of 'polish' points. Then the Send Away – I was rather proud of Bamu's Send Away and she didn't let me down. Then a slow and weary Recall to heel, followed by some mercifully brief Heel Free.

Rival competitors were watching, torn between contempt and compassion, but what did I care? I had no chance of being placed and I knew it. I only wanted to show that an Airedale could *do* all these Advanced tests, and not all our rivals had done such marvellous Send Aways. Moreover I knew we must get full marks on the Stays so long as Bamu didn't fall asleep on the Sit.

Then came Test B Scent, in which the dog has to pick from a line of identical articles the one which his handler has held for a short time. Bamu's faithful old nose couldn't be fooled on this one, and with the usual cajoling and beckoning she didn't lose much here, but to my secret amusement a lot of well-placed Alsatians and collies made a mess of the whole thing.

Nor was this all, for a good many dogs lost a great many marks on the Stays, and when the results were called 'Mrs Wright's Airedale Bamu' was actually in fourth place! Didn't we feel smug? But I never chanced putting Bamu in Test B again!

I also tried Working Trials with Bamu because I was told that polish was not so necessary, and if you got enough marks you gained a qualification which enabled you to put letters after your dog's name when sending in its show entries, and also on its pedigree when selling its offspring. Humble as ever I decided to try for the simplest test, the Certificate of Junior Merit, which had nothing to do with age but was less exhausting than the Companion Dog, Working Dog, etc.

Bamu already knew all the exercises although they were done in a slightly different order and manner and always in the open. The first attempt we failed by only one mark, and I don't think I have ever been so disappointed by anything of this nature. The second was worse in a way, but there I did have fury to help me. On that occasion dear Bamu not only scored way above the minimum required but finished fifth in a large field.

When the certificates were given out at the end I went

joyously up to receive mine, only to be told that I was not eligible for one because I was not a member of the sponsoring club. I couldn't believe my ears and protested that no such rule appeared in the schedule. Oh yes it did, they said, and showed it to me, printed in a block of minor regulations all in such tiny print that you needed a microscope to read them. What made it worse was the fact that non-members had already had to pay no less than fourteen shillings extra for the privilege of competing. As the entry fee was always much higher for these events than for ordinary shows this had meant a real difficulty for me in raising the money, and to be so unfairly excluded from the award we had earned with all this effort upset me very badly, especially as to the Alsatian club responsible it was after all nothing but a piece of printed card.

I said some very bitter words to a friend who happened to be on the committee and the next year the rule was changed, whether through her efforts or not I don't know, but in any case it was too late. I did not feel I could put Bamu through it again. She was showing her age and her sight was failing. To this day I can't think of that trial without a pang of bitterness – it became a bug that certainly knew how to bite!

Today Bamu would probably be thrown out of the ring before we had completed her heelwork. Obedience has become such a science, and competition is so keen that it is not all that uncommon for a dog to get full marks and still not be in the cards. You may well doubt such scores, but take it from me, you can believe them. Top handlers and their dogs just don't make mistakes any more.

The club which I happened to pick, however, was more concerned with helping pet owners than with open competition, thanks largely to the influence of that same lady who had answered my first phone call. Before long I was asked if I would like to try my hand at a little instructing on an approval basis.

Although it took place more than twenty years ago, I can still remember my first class. The none-too-large floor was shared by four of us aspiring instructors, each surrounded by a ring of dog owners all desperately hoping that we knew what we were doing. The noise was deafening, the procedure confused, punctuated now and then by loose dogs charging madly from group to group, disrupting some, scattering others. But at the end I at least emerged, tousled, exhausted and triumphant. Given any sort of a chance I knew I could do it. And from then on a large part of my thinking time became dedicated to working out ways to put the training gospel over to my pupils.

21

He'll do it at home

One of the first things I learnt by heart as an instructor
was the constant plaint 'He'll do it at home.' In fact one
member, herself an old hand who knew much more than I
ever did, told me that if ever she wrote a book on training,
that would be its title. Dogs who don't 'do it' at the class
will often do it at home because dogs' minds do not work
in the same way that ours do. When we teach a dog to do
an exercise in one place, with everything arranged just so
to suit a successful performance, we are teaching it that
that place and those circumstances are *part of the command*,
and this explains why so many dogs refuse to show off
their tricks to strangers. Everything isn't just right, the
command is incomplete, and the dog gets confused and
plays hard to get.

In spite of this, however, doing it at home is a healthy
move in the right direction, and if the circumstances are
varied as much as possible after this point has been
reached you will be moving towards a dog which will 'do

it' whenever and wherever required. Much less common are the dogs who will do it at class but not anywhere else. They are much more difficult to correct, and after all 'doing it' in the class is not what training is all about. It *should* become a new bond between dog and owner and an advantage to both in everyday life. Needless to say Toffee became a prime example of the difficult kind of dog.

At the bottom end of the scale are the dogs which attend steadily, week after week, without ever apparently making the slightest progress. You begin to dread their appearance because you feel you are failing their perspiring owners, until one day an owner buttonholes you and tells you how grateful he is because however wicked Mopsy may still be at the class, back in the wide world she has become a reformed character.

We have also had one or two startling successes, such as the little Cairn which did quite well in class, but which one day covered us all with glory. A friend had accidentally let him out of the car into the middle of some nasty traffic. His panic-stricken owner immediately yelled 'Down!' and he went flat just where he had landed, quite close to the car, enabling her to gather him up undamaged and almost certainly saving his life.

Even more startling was the case of Jack the Jack Russell. He was the first of his breed we had ever had at the club; in fact it was years before we had another. Jack wasn't a dog calculated to spread his breed's good name. Although very pretty he was really a nut case. His mistress brought him faithfully, week after week for about eighteen months. During the whole of that time he never once responded to a command, in fact he probably never even heard one, because he spent the entire time barking, squealing, wagging, panting and trembling at the end of his lead, too excited even to acknowledge her existence, let alone her words.

She herself did learn some useful handling principles, and with these she eventually decided to be content, ceased her attendances, and peace descended over the training class. A few months later we received a letter from her in which she told us the following story.

One very hot day she took Jack for a walk in the local park, originally the grounds of a stately home. She couldn't let him off the lead because of the groups of deer which decorate the park, and becoming tired, sat down under a tree to rest. Soon she felt sleepy, and leant back for a snooze with the loop of Jack's lead over her toe. Dozing off, she suddenly heard a scream from Jack, felt a tug at her foot and struggled up to see him hurtling down the hill towards the deer.

'Stop him! He'll kill them!' she shouted at some people in the line of fire, but they just gaped at her. In desperation she yelled the one word that came to her in her panic.

'Jack! DOWN!'

To her amazement and disbelief Jack turned at once to face her and slowly lay down and stayed on the spot until she was able to reach him and gain possession of the lead.

So far as I know it was the only time in his life that he obeyed an order, but to her it made all that eighteen months' weary work worthwhile. And we promptly removed Jack's name from the head of our list of failures!

It is often said by devotees that Obedience isn't fun any more. Since Solo's death I have had little heart for show competition so I wouldn't know. But we certainly had a lot of fun in those early days when people would come to the club with the oddest-looking treasures and give as the breed name such things as 'Woodle', 'Wittersham bull terrier' – this was obviously a straight cross between a boxer and a Labrador – or even 'Astrakan corgi'.

Once when I was doing the booking-in I took a quick glance at the new member's dog and wrote down 'Golden retriever'. The owner saw this and said in an offended tone 'He's not a retriever, he's a Border collie.' As practically anything without a pedigree was called a Border collie at that time, especially by those selling it, I let it pass, apologised, and altered the book.

But Shep grew and grew, and eventually it only needed one look at his rear elevation, with the thick straight tail and the monstrous double dew claws hanging like bunches of grapes above his back feet, to realise that at least half his parentage must have been Pyrenean Mountain Dog. Where the Border collie came in was certainly invisible to the naked eye.

Fortunately his owner was open to conviction. Just as well as the dog gave a good deal of trouble later on. Pyrenean's aren't everybody's dog even when pure bred, and when mixed with nobody knows what there's scope for an awful lot of odd traits to appear. Shep developed a habit of attacking their eighteen-year-old daughter every time she showed signs of going to bed for the night. He was cured when they insisted on his sleeping in her bedroom. It's difficult to fathom the mental processes of dogs such as this, because he was devoted to this girl at any other time. Probably it was a perverted protective instinct.

There were many memorable characters among both canine and human members of our club. I can still see the Border collie who fancied another dog's dumb-bell, and on being sent to fetch his own carefully picked up both in the form of a cross and presented them to his handler.

One of the biggest laughs I ever had at the club was when a beagle-whippet cross (which looked like a smooth fox terrier) was sent to do Test A scent for the first time without extra commands. Test A is the most junior of the three senior tests and is supposed to be worked with only one simultaneous command and signal. Tanzie had been doing this well when given encouragement and was rather thrown off her stroke to find her owner suddenly struck dumb. With one or two doubtful backward looks she went out, did a good search, selected the correct article and took it back to her handler. Or almost. With two yards still to go she hesitated and then came to a halt, looking enquiringly at him.

With commendable self control he neither spoke or moved, but just waited in the hope that she would do the usual thing and present it to him in the correct Sit position.

Tanzie felt this was very strange and wasn't at all sure of the appropriate procedure. She stood and thought for a minute and obviously decided that the wisest course was to go back to the beginning and start again. She turned, still with the article in her mouth, trotted sedately back to the group of decoys, carefully put it down in the very position she had taken it from and quietly went back at heel by her owner's left foot!

After a year or two at the club I was asked to become Secretary and we instituted a system of classes, beginning with the simplest basic exercises to the most advanced, promotion being governed solely by the results of progress tests so that nobody felt they were being kept down because their face didn't fit. Also our intake was limited to a whole class of New Dogs which we admitted every six weeks.

People get unbelievably strung up at the imminence of a progress test, and many won't turn up at all that week in order to avoid it. We had a very charming husband and wife duo who had joined us with two diminutive poodles. I stewarded in one of their first tests and was amused, on calling the husband into the ring, to see him scarlet faced, tight-lipped and perspiring with sheer tension.

'You should have taken a tranquilliser before you came out' I teased him.

'I did!' was his reply.

What would he have been like without it?

Another member was an elderly lady who was brought by an immense pile of tousled hair which proved on inspection to have a dog inside it. Chummie was absolutely fizzing with high spirits and energy, and considerably brighter than his keen but bewildered Mum.

They had just graduated to a class in which I was endeavouring to teach the members how to get their dogs down in preparation for the Down Stay.

'You can use either Flat or Down for the command,' I said, 'Pick whichever you like, but then you must stick to it.'

I got them started and then began going from one to the other to help them with any difficulties. When I came to the all-in wrestling match which represented Chummie's studies I found his owner saying 'Chummie flat! Chummie lie! Chummie down!'

I stopped and explained patiently that she must use only *one* of these commands, it didn't matter which, and passed on. To my surprise, on my second circuit of the hall the same thing was going on. Stifling the impulse to take her by both ears, I said as kindly as I could, 'You must use only one of these commands. Now which are you going to choose?'

Raising to me a flustered face which had nearly as much hair hanging over it as Chummie's, she replied 'Well, you see, he doesn't seem to understand *any* of them, so I'm trying them all!'

This dog actually got into the Advanced class and became a good worker in spite of his handicap.

We have a number of Annual Awards given at our club which are intended to encourage the members and let them know we are aware of their difficulties. One of these is for 'the handler most held back by his dog', where we feel the handling has been good but the dog exceptionally difficult. Sometimes I feel we should have one for the dog most held back by his handler. If we had then Chummie would have won it easily!

Once the New Dogs class was graced by a lady who brought her Pekinese in a basket and proceeded to do heelwork with him still inside it! Counting ten carefully the young instructor asked her to put her dog on the floor like the other dogs.

'Lollipop doesn't like to walk,' came the reply.

'God gave Lollipop four little legs, and Lollipop is going to use them!' flashed the instructor, and was rewarded by the woman stalking out and never coming back again.

To this day I can't imagine how she thought Lollipop was going to benefit by a training class if he never got out of his basket. Perhaps he begged nicely for a sweetie and she thought we would like to see him do it.

22

Toffee the trained dog

Toffee wasn't one of those who do it at home, unless perhaps in the garden with no hope of escape. But at the club she spread sweetness and light. She adored the club and thought the training was a scream.

She was very useful in the New Dogs class. Nervous first-nighters clutching aggressive dogs would cling desperately to them and hoarsely beg me to keep away when they saw her coming – she was usually the biggest dog there. They would look at me in frozen horror when I told them that their dog wouldn't fight her, but even as they stammered their protests they would become aware that their dog had stopped snarling, a glassy look had come into its eyes and its tail was actually beginning to wag. I'm afraid that with many this alone put me into the mystical dogwoman class.

It didn't take a dog of Toff's brain power long to grasp the whole Obedience schedule. Stephen worked very hard on her and was praised by more than one outside judge for the quality of his handling. Toffee bore it all with her typical 'You carry on as you like, it doesn't bother me' good humour. But knowing the schedule was one thing, doing it quite another.

Toffee had a vast capacity for boredom. For instance, she would often stroll in on the Recall while enjoying a series of gargantuan yawns which would have got a serviceman a month in the glasshouse. She always enjoyed her educational nights out, but praise given for work well done she received with contempt. She preferred to put a little zest into things by extempore variations on the schedule, and got quite a name for her brilliance in this direction, as when she finished the scent exercise by doing a kind of lap of honour with the article so that onlookers should be in no doubt that it was the correct one. She got applause for this innovation, which pleased her very much.

Sometimes she would present the dumb-bell meekly, but to the judge or steward instead of Stephen. Once when we had a guest instructor she did a splendid Retrieve, but as she sat in front of Stephen everyone could plainly see the ends of the dumb-bell whizzing round as she twirled it with great speed and dexterity on her tongue.

It occurs to me after all these years that it was done so fast and with so much skill . . . could she possibly have been practising it in private and saving it for a suitable occasion? I wouldn't put it past her, she always liked to get the laughs, and probably remembered the success of her front-end Sit in that early class.

Her talent as an actress also came in useful – to her. Stephen, always a glutton for punishment, had entered her in a Novice class at an Open Show. She put up her usual fair-to-awful performance until it came to the Retrieve. Stephen threw the dumb-bell and tried to send her out after it . . . She immediately went into an exquisite act, most sensitively performed, making it quite clear to all beholders that she hadn't the slightest idea as to what was required of her.

Fetch? What's that? If I only knew what you wanted me

to do, adored boss, I'd do it. Like a shot. But whatever can you mean?

You could almost feel sorry for her, poor bewildered little dog, dithering about the ring, gazing anxiously into Stephen's face. No doubt the whole ringside did. No doubt they were also thinking 'That boy's a fool. He's never taught that dog the exercise.' But my sympathy was all with Stephen. He had to fetch the dumb-bell himself in the end. Twenty-five marks went bang to join the other dozen or so she had already lost, and he towed her out of the ring choking with fury.

He took her into an empty room away from the main arena, where she obligingly did three perfect Retrieves one after another just to show him it had only been her little joke. She must have wondered what had happened to his sense of humour, because he was definitely *not* amused.

Not the least of her infuriating tricks was the way in which now and again she would work very well indeed, and we came to the conclusion that in doing so she was merely rubbing salt into our wounds by proving that her normal intransigence was deliberate and not the result of ignorance or incapability.

Once she and Stephen actually came fifth in a large Open Novice class, with a score of 99½ out of 100. For as long as we live, neither Stephen or I will ever have a more startling triumph. The card was promptly framed and hung on the wall to the wonder and disbelief of all behol-ders.

Toffee did become crashingly bored with her weekly training routine, and with her eye always on the main chance was quite pleased when a badly cut foot got her excused for three or four weeks. She obviously thought this wasn't long enough, and for *three months* after the foot was completely healed she developed a paralysing limp as soon as she was taken on to the training floor.

It was piteous to watch her. There were many disap-proving faces, and more than one instructor offered to excuse her. Stephen's stock reply, 'She's all right, she's only acting,' was not very well received. But expressions changed abruptly when at the end of the class Steve would say 'Coming home Toff?' Then she would be miraculously cured and rush madly round the hall trying to beat poor little Bamu into a pulp in her joy.

She knew how to play it for sympathy, too. You could practically hear her bones creak as she crawled painfully across the floor on a long long Recall and sank brokenly into the Sit position in front of Steve. There were always a few reproachful 'Aaaahs'. Really she developed a split personality, becoming so docile in class that it looked as if we were beating her six times a day. But she was only like this at the hall and out of sight of green grass. In every other situation she was really much the same insouciant old hell.

At the club she was much admired. I well remember a new member coming up to me after Toffee had been demonstrating some exercises and telling me that his ambition was one day to own 'a dog as good as that one'. I managed to smile but was fortunately rendered speechless.

One of Toffee's quirks which had an adverse effect on every single exercise was her renowned slow Sit. It was a pity this was never filmed for posterity, as she must have set up a world record for the longest time taken to get bot to floor without actually stopping on the way down. This record would still be standing today.

One day I had the chance of going to a lecture by a German who had trained dogs to patrol the Russian border. Of course I jumped at the opportunity and enjoyed the lecture very much, although a lot of it didn't seem too applicable to the problems of British owners. He replied to a question from a lady as to how to cure her toy poodle's nerves with the advice that it should be trained to do man work!

However, he was very knowledgeable, so when question time came I thought I would ask him if he had that Magic Word which might transform Toffee into a normal animal. He seemed interested in her case and asked a lot of questions about her, such as what was her breed, age, sex life, record as a mother, and what her health and guarding propensities were like.

I answered all these queries truthfully, and stood waiting painfully for that reply which might transform all our lives. He drew himself up sternly and his answer was annihilating.

'Madam,' he said, 'You have the perfect dog for training!'

And so another balloon of hope was burst. I took it philosophically; after all, it wasn't likely that they had any dogs like Toff on the Russian frontier. She would have spent half her time belting all over the steppes or whatever they call their wide open spaces out there, and the other half fraternising with the Russians and getting a taste for their food. I fear that when she *did* get home she would have succumbed to what the lecturer described as 'just a leetle injection'.

What no expert ever seemed to grasp was that Toff's reactions to stimuli just weren't the same as other dogs'. She was like a chocolate-bar machine which on receipt of the correct coin insists on shelling out gob-stoppers, aspirins or hairclips instead. You put the right thing in but there was no saying what you were going to get out. She was born out of her time, too late for the Goon Show and too early for Monty Python's Flying Circus. If there is truth in reincarnation, I'd love to know what she's doing now.

23
Top Dogs

Although our fees were low, such was the popularity of our club that we found we had a quite respectable surplus in the bank. The Committee thought that this should be used in some way to benefit the members, and I suggested a monthly news sheet and offered to run it.

Thus was born *Top Dogs*, which ran for nearly four years before pressure of other work forced me to give it up. To my sorrow, no one else felt they could carry it on.

The name was suggested by my daughter as a temporary title to be used till someone thought of something better. It was frankly stolen from the slogan (then fairly new) 'Top People read *The Times*'. One of the first things we did was to run a competition to find an alternative, with members voting on titles suggested, but in the event the vote was overwhelmingly in favour of retaining the original name.

Since our financial surplus was not unlimited we had to keep the costs of production to the minimum. Filled with that boundless confidence which is only engendered by total ignorance I undertook to produce it on a duplicator if the club would buy one.

The Committee agreed and rashly left it to me to choose one. Looking back I still don't see that I could have followed a wiser course than the one I did, which was to go to a firm of office suppliers, admit that I knew nothing of duplicators and ask their guidance in choosing one. They were, after all, a reputable firm, and had been supplying all our requirements in the way of stationery for quite a long time.

So I suppose I was just unlucky in the salesman who fell to my lot. He didn't show a lot of enthusiasm, or sales drive either, because he eventually sold me one of their cheapest machines. Funds would certainly have stretched to a better one, and it would have been money well spent, as my prize turned out to be a non-self-inking model – and oh what a world of woe I let the production staff in for by that single fact. I speak from experience, for Steve and I were that staff for a long time, and thought our persons and clothes would never be free of ink again.

I had decided on a publication date of the first club night in each month. I'm not sure now how big our circulation was at first, sixty copies perhaps, but demand rapidly increased and at the close it was about a hundred and fifty. Each copy consisted of about half a dozen roneoed sheets, (printed on one side only because the ink always went right through the paper) stapled at one corner.

About a third of the first page was taken up with a would-be ornamental heading, with the name *Top Dogs* prominently displayed in lettering which varied monthly in all shapes from rococo to ultra modern, and usually a picture too, picked out by me on the stencil with a stylo and usually drawn by me too. Beneath it would be such official items as reports of Committee meetings and show reviews, or perhaps a scoop in the shape of some triumph scored by a member.

Inside would be the results of the regular Progress Tests, with some remarks by their judges; dates of tests to come and other approaching events; and a variety of infor-

225

mation about the club and its activities, rounded off with unfailing regularity by the ever-necessary plea to members not to let their dogs foul the hall or nearby approaches.

All of this except the judges' critiques was written by me, and as I often contributed general articles and the odd verse, it happened more than once that I wrote the whole thing, then duplicated it and finished off by stapling the whole edition to boot. This was an uncommon occurrence, however, as my bitter howls of complaint on these occasions usually elicited a satisfactory response in the shape of a sheaf of contributions which enriched the next four or five numbers considerably.

We were fortunate in having a number of members who were specialists in so far as they were faithful to their favourite breeds and had bred at least some puppies. It seemed to me a natural consequence to initiate a series of articles entitled 'What do they See in Them?' in which one of these breeder-members would do his or her best to answer this question each month. This series was popular and lasted quite a long time, giving a good lead for what I hoped would be the most rewarding aspect of our news-sheet – the lighter side, which was to clothe the bare bones of facts and fixtures, dates, reports and informative articles.

Nor was I disappointed. For a start I got an offer from a member, Pauline, who owned a very eccentric Scottie named Tina, to cut the stencils, and in the process she became so keen that she also contributed a lot of articles, usually very funny and sometimes too Rabelaisian to go in without severe censorship.

Pauline, in her private capacity as a wife and mother, also produced two male offspring over the period that *Top Dogs* was in production, a complication which was often quite obvious in her work. One evening, for instance, she left her dog at home and arrived with her typewriter instead, and when she should have been training she cut the current month's stencils.

The importunities of her offspring often had an unfortunate effect on her typing and spelling, and she endured much sly leg-pulling on the subject before writing the following letter to me, ostensibly not for publication, but I sneaked it in by cutting the stencil for it myself.

Dear Mada,m

    Your carres pondent, Stephen WrigltS atteges thet the Magazien TopDogs id typ ted ian; ccuratley. I wish to deny thos. If an errot shoudl accosinally creep in then Iavn only say pehrpls he sould cosidtr the followint. It is 7 yewrs or xxmore sinve I was in emptyment as a sbft—hand typist. txhereofore am not really in practie;. Also I thonk he woulrd fine it difficult to type with a TYprewrite wikl a will of tiw own balanced on his knews wxbile attemying to restrain a 10 momth old potential suididex form cbwint thro8th and electirc fle x, ramming the dogw tail down itw throqt, LAuntching itwelf into ouyer space, x tattooingt itwelf with xmy Briro, making will a 9med grobs at tye stencil and typew5iter and pxlaing his faoritt game of Getting on Mymmus Nervers.'

    In cincluwion I have berro accuwed os writingthe article on Page 6 of the sEptemre issu. I thinr that infuxore no anonon onoyous work shoule be acceptec.

    As the afore mentionw baby gow now upset a set or miniturw chess man allover the floor, I must come to adtop and rettrive tbb. beore itis tll late.

    Yowrs fstlrully,

        Pauline H. (Scootie Tina)

(shortly t o be reregisterd as Travesty of XTraining)

227

We also tried to include a poem in every issue and soon got complaints if there were none. Again Pauline and I wrote most of them, but we did get some from other sources too, notably one of our junior members, a schoolgirl who had a fine Dalmatian. Her standard was so high that I am pleased to recall that all the editorial staff thought she had the makings of a good poet. Pleased, because that's exactly what she became, and has since read some of her work on the radio. It would be nice to think that her early successes in our humble rag helped to encourage her to go on to better things.

As we began to run out of contributions for the 'What Do They See in Them?' series I felt we might include a few words from one of our canine members, and published the following 'interview'.

Why I like Siamese Cats

By T. F. Toffee Nut in an interview with Our Special Correspondent.

The club well of owner-breeders having apparently run dry it occurred to us to ask Pamela Walker if she would care to contribute a few words on Siamese cats for a change. Pam, however, said that it would have to be entitled 'Why I *hate* Siamese cats' and added that she daren't do it 'because Mummy would kill me'.

Not wishing to unleash any surging passions in the Walker household, we were on the point of giving up the idea when we remembered that we have another member with strong views on these animals, who is always only too ready to talk.

This member, of course, is none other than T. F. Toffee Nut, the well-known Dog. Hastily making circular scribbling motions with our Biro to get it working, we hurried along to interview her. Toffee Nut, known affectionately to her intimates as 'that ghastly dog' or 'you old stinker', went on the stage at the age of four months, when she played the juvenile lead in a school play, and has since travelled extensively, mostly alone. She has made a detailed study of back gardens in the Bickley area and has got through, over, under, round or just out of, every known type of fence. She is well known for her brilliant extempore variations on the Obedience schedule and is an authority on cats of every kind.

We found her lying on her back in a graceful S curve, occupying a good deal of carpet and looking remarkably hairy. She opened one eye and extended a paw about a yard towards us, drew it back languidly and shut her eye again.

'We have heard,' we said ingratiatingly, 'that your ability to relax is only equalled by your ability to run.'

She sighed modestly.

'And that you run as fast and as far as ninety degrees as you do when it's freezing.'

'Of course.' She sounded surprised.

'But isn't that very hot?'

'I really don't have time to notice. Besides, the breeze you know, at that speed – much more refreshing than standing about.'

'We really came to ask you about Siamese cats.'

A sort of convulsion occurred and she was battering herself against the window before we had even seen her move.

'Where is it? Let me out!! Yowww!!!'

'Please be calm, Miss Nut. There is a Siamese living only two doors away, I understand?'

'I only want to see what it's made of! I swear I'll give it back afterwards . . .'

The French windows gave way. So did the fence.

The interview was over.

(T. F. The Famous)

Yes, we did have a lot of fun with our News-sheet, and during the four years it ran I think it added a very enjoyable extra dimension to club membership.

Unfortunately, as my personal circumstances changed I had to give it up. Pauline, up to her eyes in motherhood, had long since stopped doing the stencils and was equally unable to take over the editorship. No one else wanted the job, and so *Top Dogs* died. But it was fun while it lasted, and I shall always remember it with affection as another happy experience which came to me through my dogs.

24

Trials and triumphs of a secretary

Acting as Secretary took a lot of time and patience apart from my chores for *Top Dogs* and the time spent in attendance at the class – and as far as I can remember I never missed that once all the six years that I was doing the job.

One of the worst things was the amount of time I was forced to spend on the telephone. I was continually getting calls, not only from people who wanted to join, or other committee members discussing club business, but from members who seemed to think I had hours to spend chewing over their own darling problem dogs.

I was genuinely willing to help if I could, but most of them really only wanted to talk and were often very difficult to get rid of, because no matter what ploy I suggested they could always give reasons why it wouldn't work with Fido. I got to dread one particular voice, and one day went into such a trance of hopeless misery on my end of the wire that I became quite mesmerised and gave up all hope of escape.

Did I say gave up all hope? Well I came out of my trance to find myself upstairs making the beds! At some point in the monologue I must simply have put the phone down and gone about my business. I wonder if I uttered my thoughts aloud as I did so? I hoped the voice would think we had simply been cut off, but at any rate it never rang again!

I did score a bulls-eye one day with an elderly lady who had taken to her heart a young and very lively male Labrador. She and her husband were quite unable to tire him out enough to make him settle down even after a walk.

I asked her if he had any toys and she said yes, he had plenty of toys, balls, slippers and so forth. I told her these things were not enough for such a dog and advised her to ask her garage for an old inner tube and to hang it from a branch in her garden at the dog's own height.

This was a success beyond my wildest dreams. Apparently Pedro spent every waking minute apart from mealtimes locked in combat with this object, shaking it until it banged wildly against his backside, and then turning on it in fury for being so impertinent. In this way he would lash himself into a state of great excitement and eventually stagger back to the house, legs rubbery and tongue hanging out.

Of such lucky stabs are great reputations made! I think that couple would have believed anything I told them after that.

Another success came to me in an even stranger way. I was out with my dogs when I met a lady who happened to be in my class at the club, with her absolutely scrumptious Great Dane puppy, brinded like the tiger, almost full-grown and very bouncy. We talked, but with apologies I told her I must call Toffee, who needed to be checked up on about every ninety seconds if any sort of contact was to be maintained. Toffee, however, had already taken advantage of my temporary preoccupation and was nowhere to be seen. My pupil was very concerned about her non-appearance and confessed that she was having a similar problem with Loppylugs. She stayed with me, worrying, for the next three-quarters of an hour.

231

Here, I thought, was a perfect case of Physician heal thyself. In self-defence I told her what Toff was like and tried to be nonchalant, while inwardly cursing. Finally Toffee reappeared, probably curious to see what was going on, as Loppy had remained on lead in case he decided she was having a better walk than he was and joined her. I was in no mood for recriminations and devoted my energies to coaxing her in. This was seldom any trouble since Toff had decided to give herself up, and she came and sat meekly at my feet so that I could put her lead on, which I did with an affectionate pat.

To my surprise my pupil was tremendously impressed by this! First because Toffee had indulged in no last-yard dodging at the sight of the lead, and second, because I had actually practised what I preached and refrained from beating her to a pulp as soon as I laid hands on her. I pointed out that the first was the direct result of the second, and that no dog should ever be punished for coming, no matter how homicidal the handler may feel.

'Oh, I know that,' she said, 'but I didn't think you'd actually be able to resist it after she'd been so naughty.' I hope that Loppy benefited from this incident and that she subsequently had less trouble with the Recall.

Not that my word always carried much weight. I was looking gloomily one night at two identical dogs of a certain breed and thinking how ghastly they were. One of them was owned by a young man who was continually taking up a good deal of my time asking for advice which he never seemed to follow. The dog seemed to be getting worse, and although still a puppy was in my opinion unreliable in temper. On this occasion his owner was again asking me what he should do with him.

'If you got about a third of his weight off him you'd have less to cope with,' I said nastily, 'and he might behave a bit better too.'

'He's not fat,' came the indignant answer. (They never are!)

'I'm afraid he is,' I replied.

'He's not!'

'I'm sorry, owners often can't see this because the dog is

with them all the time, but take my word for it. He's fat.'

'Do you think you know better than his breeder, then, who's been breeding these dogs for forty years and has the best in the country?'

'If he says he's not fat, then yes, I do.'

The other identical dog chose this minute to make a vicious unprovoked attack on an inoffensive class-mate, fortunately foiled by the instructor, who hadn't taken her eye off him since the class began. The startling likeness struck me again.

'Are Ginger and Sandy litter brothers?' I asked, hoping to lower the temperature a little.

His face lit up. 'Funny you should ask that. They aren't actually litter brothers but they have the same mother and father, only Ginger is six weeks older than Sandy.'

'Don't you mean six months?'

'No. We've compared pedigrees. Sandy is just six weeks younger than Ginger.'

Shaken to my very core I could only reply

'That's what I call a brood bitch!'

These were complete novices of course, and being taken for a ride by an unscrupulous dealer. There is less excuse for the would-be doggy. Helping to deliver a first litter for a new fancier I was somewhat taken aback to be told after the birth of the sixth pup 'That's enough, we don't want any more now.' The bitch had other ideas and went on to produce nine.

A day or two later, a little light-headed from the avalanche but rallying strongly, he told me impressively that the main trouble with running on a bitch puppy for show was that one couldn't be sure whether it might not turn out to be a monorchid. As monorchidism (or more correctly, unilateral cryptorchidism) means the descent of only one testicle into the scrotum, I felt he might have rested easy on that score. The more disillusioned among doggy circles will not be surprised to learn that this man was judging within a year or two of uttering this deathless statement.

One expects less of pet people, and I feel nothing but affection for the man who brought his very handsome, but monorchid, dog in for a trim and told me that the vet had said he was a very fine dog except that he only had one orchestra!

It's well over twenty years now since Toff towed me into our first training class. She is long gone, and Bamu too, but Bamu's descendants at a remove of several generations still accompany me to class, and I am still a member of the same club, my spiritual home. Most of the human members I met in those early days have also departed, but a few remain, and so does the happy family atmosphere which has made it so enjoyable through all those years.

We still have progress tests, we still have parties and the occasional match with another club. We have our laughs and we have our tragedies too, both canine and human . . .

Sunny was attacked repeatedly by a Great Dane in her very first training class and was put off formal Obedience for life. Socks, a natural clown, was so excitable in the ring and took so much handling that after I worked her in one class at a show a ringsider, laughing like a drain, came up and shook my hand, saying that he'd never seen anything like it and I ought to get a special award for pluck! Sunny's daughter Sadie showed a lot of promise but was unluckily put off the Retrieve by the pain from an injured leg. I did get her to Retrieve eventually, but only after another three years had gone by, by which time it was too late.

Sadie's daughter Storm has come the nearest of my dogs to replacing Solo. She was an amazingly precocious puppy, opening her eyes at nine days instead of the usual fourteen, and pulling her brothers' tails while they were still blind. I have read that a puppy's intelligence is not 'switched on' until it is three weeks old, but at two weeks Storm would sit at the front of the box and wave a paw at me when she saw me coming. I adored her from the word go and was very sad because I felt I had too many dogs already to keep her. When I was selling the puppies I had an enquiry for her from a woman who tried to beat me down in price. I absolutely refused, as she was such a gorgeous puppy and the only bitch in the litter. Three days later the woman rang again to say she would have her at my price. With triumph in my heart I was able to tell her that as I had sold Spangles (from a quite unexpected enquiry) I would be able to keep Storm myself!

Storm grew to be very big and strong, nearly as big as Toffee. She had all her adult teeth, great strong white ones, at exactly five months of age, and developed a truly wonderful character, willing, co-operative and loving. I enjoyed training her as I thought I would never enjoy it again, and it is entirely my fault that she has never progressed beyond Test A.

One day I had her and her daughter Saffron, then seven months old and still very much at her mother's tail, in the Bedgebury Pinetum, where we had gone with a neighbour's little girl. The dogs had run on ahead. I heard some commotion, and going round a corner found a middle-aged couple in a great state, with the man lashing out at the dogs with his camera while they were jumping up under the impression that this was a game.

I called them off and apologised as I came up. But the man was in a fury and slated me for having my dogs loose, although this is allowed in the Pinetum. Surprised, but not wanting any trouble, I offered, if he would tell me which way they were going, to go somewhere else, but this wouldn't do. He said we would be a nuisance to everybody wherever we went – in spite of the fact that it is a big place and seemed to be deserted but for ourselves. Rather nettled, I pointed out that they were trained dogs.

'Trained dogs!' he said, 'Why, they won't even come when they're called.'

'Oh no?' I said. Storm and Saffron had lost interest and were pootling about among some bushes some thirty feet away. 'Stormy come!' I called, and dear old Storm, as I knew she would, immediately made a bee-line for me. I knew too that she would sit as she reached me, so at the psychological moment I rapped out 'Sit!' She promptly slid into the sit at my feet. 'Flat!' I cried, and she went down – all, you notice, on a single command. 'Now Stay,' I said as I stepped away from her, and then some demon made me add (I really don't know what put it into my head) 'and when you get up, bite him!'

This was really my bit of fun, but whoops – he had his shoe off to defend himself! After all, poor chap, she'd done everything else I told her, and he could hardly know that she wouldn't do that too! His wife, incidentally, said nothing from first to last. I have a feeling that she was secretly enjoying the whole thing. I hope so!

I think it is very sad that so many people are trying to stop dogs and their owners enjoying our open spaces. Sad not only for dogs and their owners but for children and the whole community. One day soon I hope this will be realised and the pendulum swing back again. After all, what good is a park, no matter how free from pollution by dogs, if children and the elderly dare not venture into it for fear of attack from muggers and other thugs? This is beginning to be the case in some places, and personally I think the disciples of cruelty and violence have things made too easy for them already. A regular company of dog walkers in all weathers is a free and good protection for the innocent in these lonely places.

All the same, dog owners must do their part too. They must realise that not everybody cares for the close proximity of other people's dogs, and they must keep their pets under proper control at all times. Dogs should not be allowed to roam, and all dogs should receive a basic education making them good citizens of our twentieth century world.

All over the country there are training clubs, where a course of minimum Obedience will make a great difference to a dog. It's also one of the best ways to enjoy a dog, be it angel or devil!

25

Honorary dog

There are many other kinds of dog training besides Obedience, ranging from house training, lead training and car training to police work, mountain rescue and guiding. I'm proud to say that one of Sunny's daughters, Star, who was Sadie's litter sister, became a Guide Dog. She was trained by Stephen, who went into the Guide Dogs, (probably, I felt, on the rebound from Toffee!) However, as this is an account of what dogs have meant in my own life I will say no more about these specialist fields in which I have no personal experience.

To the end of my life I shall have a gallery of remembered pictures to amuse my idle hours . . .

Scamp carrying a long bough through a narrow gap at full gallop, by expertly turning his head at the crucial point.

Digger dancing with the fairies in the dusky garden.

Jane bustling along, chrysanthemum ears flying.

Bamu talking, to tell me Pud was on the table.

237

Toffee sitting companionably on Naomi's stomach on the sunbaked lawn, while eating green gooseberries out of a saucepan.

Chai moving Naomi's little donkey.

Peggy with her white bushy rear sticking industriously out of a rabbit hole.

Solo stopping on the Halt with her paw on my foot.

Sunny the champion kisser with her ready smile and readier lick.

Socks searching for lost puppies in the long grass.

Sadie industriously trying and trying again until she discovered just how to open a door from either side.

Storm miraculously curing a friend's bad back by knocking him clean off his stool with one well-aimed leap.

And so on and so on.

In my earliest years I drove my mother mad by preferring the kitchen floor with the dog for company rather than the elegance of the front parlour with my visiting relations. Now, fifty years on, I live like Dr Dolittle in a little house with a big garden and arrange everything for the comfort and convenience of my animal family.

Marriage and motherhood have intervened, but I regret to say that I can still remember dates best by relating events to the lives of my dogs – I never forget *their* dates. But of course, comfort and convenience for my dogs actually add up to comfort and convenience for *me* in my constant dealings with them.

But how nice to be personally needed by the whelping bitch. How nice to be able to play it by ear with the resultant puppies, because something in me seems to know what they need. How wonderful to see the awakening puppy minds deciding that the human race must be all right because they feel so comfortable in contact with me.

How nice to see the upset, mishandled poodle subside unbelievingly into quiescence as he realises from my almost imperceptible signs and signals that I am not to be feared, and may even become a Good Thing in his life.

Honorary Dog? Can you smile at a dog in the street and get a friendly wag in return? It doesn't happen to me every time, but often enough to make me feel one of the gang.

Looking back I realise that dogs, and especially my Airedales, have given me more joy and pleasure than any other single factor in my life. Whether that is good or bad I leave it to others to decide.

If I am eccentric who cares? Certainly I don't, and am proud to sign this book. . . .

Dora Wright,
Honorary Dog.